The Excel Essentials Quiz Book

M.L. HUMPHREY

TITLES BY M.L. HUMPHREY

.

CONTENTS

AUTHOR'S NOTE

The Excel Essentials Quiz Book combines the content from four separate titles: *The Excel for Beginners Quiz Book, The Intermediate Excel Quiz Book, The 50 Useful Excel Functions Quiz Book,* and *The 50 More Excel Functions Quiz Book.*

Because the original versions of *The 50 Useful Excel Functions Quiz Book* and *The 50 More Excel Functions Quiz Book* contained identical quizzes related to formula and function basics, the two books have been edited and combined into one section of this book titled *The 100 Excel Functions Quiz Book.*

The Excel for Beginners Quiz Book

M.L. HUMPHREY

CONTENTS

INTRODUCTION

This is a companion book written to complement *Excel for Beginners* by M.L. Humphrey and is geared towards those who are already familiar with the content covered in that book who now want to test their knowledge through quizzes or to those who learn better from a question and answer format.

For each chapter in *Excel for Beginners* there is a set of questions meant to test your knowledge of the information that was covered in the chapter.

The first section of the book just has the questions, the next section of the book has the questions as well as the answers. There is also a bonus section that contains five exercises where you can test your knowledge of the various functions by applying them to specific real-life scenarios.

I encourage you to try to do each exercise first without looking at the solutions, since in the real world you'll be faced with a problem that needs solved and no one will be there to tell you how to solve it. However, I would also encourage you to have Excel open as you work each exercise so you can use the help functions within Excel to find what you need. Don't feel like you need to memorize every task in Excel in order to use it effectively. You just need to know what's possible and then what keywords or phrasing to use to help you find the information that will let you perform the right task.

Alright, then. Let's start with the first quiz.

QUIZZES

TERMINOLOGY QUIZ

1. In an Excel worksheet what are generally identified by letters that run across the top of the worksheet?

    a. Columns

    b. Rows

    c. Cells

    d. Other

2. In an Excel worksheet what are generally identified by numbers that run along the left-hand side of the worksheet?

    a. Columns

    b. Rows

    c. Cells

    d. Other

3. What is a cell?

4. How do you know what cell or cell(s) you have selected?

5. In general, what does left-clicking do?

6. In general, what does right-clicking do?

7. What is the difference between a worksheet and a workbook in Excel?

8. What is the formula bar?

9. What is a scroll bar?

10. How can you use a scroll bar?
   a. Click on the bar and drag.
   b. Click on the space to either side of the bar.
   c. Click on the arrows at the top and bottom or on each end of the scroll bar space.
   d. All of the above.

11. With a scroll bar if you want to move outside of the area where you've already entered information, which method should you use?

12. Name two ways that you can select cells in a worksheet.

13. What is a dropdown menu?

14. What is a dialogue box?

15. How can you access a dialogue box?

ABSOLUTE BASICS QUIZ

1. What is the Ctrl shortcut you can use to save a file?

2. Which of the following methods works to open an existing Excel file:

> a. Double-click on the file name where it's stored on your computer
>
> b. Open Excel and choose the file name from the list under Recent on the left-hand side or navigate to the file location by clicking on Open Other Workbooks at the bottom of the page.
>
> c. If you're already in Excel, go to File and then choose Open from the left-hand side menu and then choose a file name from under Recent Workbooks or navigate to the file you want using the Computer option.
>
> d. All of the above.

3. What is the difference between Save and Save As?

4. Discuss why you might save a file as an .xls file type instead of an .xlsx file type.

5. Name three ways to save a file.

6. How can you delete an existing Excel file?

7. How can you rename an existing Excel file?

8. What issue should you be aware of if you move or rename an Excel file that you recently used?

NAVIGATING EXCEL QUIZ

1. When you open a new Excel file, what cell and worksheet does it open to?

2. When you open an existing Excel file, what cell and worksheet does it open to?

3. Name two ways you could use to get to Cell B6 if you were in Cell A1?

4. What does the Shift key do? What does Shift + Tab do?

5. In a worksheet that has a lot of data in it, what is a quick way to scroll down a large number of rows or to scroll over a large number of columns?

6. What is one very important thing you need to remember when using scrollbars to navigate an Excel worksheet?

7. Name two ways to move to a different worksheet than the one you're currently in.

8. What does using the F2 key do?

9. Name two ways to insert a cell into a worksheet.

10. What do the different insert cell options (shift cells right, shift cells down, entire row, and entire column) do?

11. Name three ways you can insert a row or column into a worksheet.

12. How do you select an entire row or column?

13. How do you insert a new worksheet into an Excel workbook?

14. How do you delete a cell in a worksheet?

15. What is the problem you might run into when you either insert a cell or cells or delete a cell or cells from a worksheet that has existing data?

16. How do you delete a column or row?

17. How do you delete a worksheet?

18. How do you rename a worksheet?

INPUTTING YOUR DATA QUIZ

1. What is the most basic way to input data in a cell in an Excel worksheet?

2. Which of the following are bad ways of inputting data in an Excel worksheet?

    a. Not labeling each column of your data.

    b. Breaking up your data entries with summary entries.

    c. Allowing users to enter data in any way and any format they want.

    d. Using a lot of free text entry fields.

    e. All of the above.

3. What is a best practice when handling a data set that you need to analyze?

4. What does Ctrl + Z do?

5. What does Ctrl + Y do?

6. If you have to make a large number of entries in a column in Excel that have a limited number of values (say, book, CD, and video), what's an easy trick for entering that information that will save you a lot of time?

7. Does auto-suggested text work with numbers?

8. Name two ways to copy the contents of a cell.

9. Name two ways to cut the contents of a cell from its current location.

10. Name two ways to paste the contents of a cell into a new location.

11. When it comes to formulas, what is the difference between Copying the contents of a cell and Cutting the contents of a cell?

12. What does using the $ sign in a formula do?

13. What does Paste Special – Values do?

14. What does Paste Special – Transpose do?

15. How can you display the contents of a cell as text without Excel trying to convert it into a date or formula?

16. How do you tell Excel that you're entering a formula into a cell?

17. How can you include line breaks within a cell in Excel (since hitting enter will just take you to the next cell)?

18. How can you delete data you've entered into a cell without deleting the cell?

19. What does Find do?

20. What does Replace do?

21. What is the danger of using Replace?

22. How do you access Find and Replace?

23. If you want to have a list of 250 entries that repeat the days of the week (Monday, Tuesday, Wednesday, etc.) what is the easiest way to do that?

24. What does Freeze Panes do?

25. How do you Freeze Panes?

26. What is one thing to be careful of when using Freeze Panes?

FORMATTING QUIZ

1. What are the Ctrl shortcuts for bolding, italics, and underlining?

2. What are the six basic cell alignment choices you have available to you?

3. How do you align text within a cell?

4. If you want to change the angle of text, how do you do that?

5. What are two other ways to bold text other than using a Ctrl shortcut?

6. What are two other ways to italicize text other than using a Ctrl shortcut?

7. What are two other ways to underline text other than using a Ctrl shortcut?

8. If you have selected text that is partially formatted in bold, italic, or underline and partially not, what will happen

when you click on the B, I, or U for bold, italic, or underline formatting?

9. When should you choose the style of border that you want to use for a given cell?

10. How can you put a diagonal border line through a cell?

11. Name two ways to apply a standard border to a cell.

12. If you just want a simple border around all of your cells, what's the best border option to use?

13. To put a darker perimeter border around a range of cells, what default option can you choose?

14. How do you clear all borders from around a cell or cells?

15. How do you add background color to a cell?

16. If you need to use a custom fill color or custom font color, how do you do this?

17. Name three ways to adjust the width of a column.

18. How can you adjust all of your column widths at once?

19. How do you select all cells in a worksheet?

20. Name three ways to adjust the height of a row.

21. How can you adjust all of your row heights at once?

22. How do you get text to wrap to the next line?

23. Name three ways you can apply currency formatting to a cell or range of cells.

24. Name two ways you can apply date formatting to a cell or range of cells.

25. What is one thing to be careful of when using dates in Excel?

26. Name two ways you can change the font used in a cell or range of cells.

27. Name four ways to change the size of the font used in a cell or range of cells.

28. How do you change the color of the text in a cell or range of cells?

29. If you've placed a dark fill color into a cell, what font color might you want to use?

30. What does Merge & Center do?

31. When might you want to use Merge & Center?

32. How do you Merge & Center a range of cells?

33. If you want to format a range of cells as a number with four decimal places, how would you do that?

34. How do you format a number as a percentage?

35. If you have the number .10 what is that as a percentage?

36. What does the Format Painter allow you to do?

37. How do you use the Format Painter?

38. What would happen if you click on the Format Painter tool and then try to use the arrow keys to navigate to the

cell where you want to apply that formatting?

39. How can you apply formatting to multiple cells that are not touching without having to go through the whole Format Painter process each time?

MANIPULATING YOUR DATA QUIZ

1. What does Sorting do?

2. Do you need to have a header row to sort data?

3. If your data does have a header row, what do you need to make sure you do when you are telling Excel how to sort your data?

4. What will happen if your data has a header row but Excel doesn't know that?

5. Should you include a summary row in your sort?

6. Name three ways to sort a range of data.

7. If the sort options that you see are Column A, Column B, Column C, etc. what does this mean?

8. What order should you list your sort criteria in?

9. If you want to sort text in an alphabetical order, which sort options should you choose?

10. If you want to sort numbers from largest to smallest, which sort options should you choose?

11. If you have a range that contains days of the week or months of the year, what sort options should you choose?

12. If you added a sort level that you don't need, how do you remove it?

13. How do you change the order in which your data will be sorted when you have multiple sort criteria listed?

14. What are some issues to be aware of when sorting?

15. What should you do if you sort data and realize you made a mistake?

16. What does filtering do?

17. How do you turn on filtering?

18. If you add a new column of data, will filtering extend to that new column?

19. How will you know when you have filtering turned on?

20. Once you've turned on filtering, how do you filter a specific column?

21. In recent versions of Excel, what options do you have for filtering data?

22. Using filtering, if you just want to see two or three specific entries in a column but have a large number of different values that are possible in that column, what's a quick trick to do that?

23. Using filtering, if you want to see all of the entries that contain the word "USA", how would you do that?

24. Using filtering, if you want to see all of the entries that have red text, how would you do that?

25. Using filtering, if you want to see all of the entries with a numerical value greater than 100, how would you do that?

26. How can you tell when your worksheet values have already been filtered?

27. How can you tell which columns have filtering in place?

28. How do you remove filtering from a specific column?

29. How do you remove filtering from all columns in a worksheet?

30. How do you turn off filtering?

31. How do you tell Excel that you want to use a function?

32. What is the function you can use to sum a range of values?

33. What is the function you can use to multiply a range of values?

34. Is there a function for subtracting values?

35. Is there a function for dividing values?

36. What is the symbol you can use to add two values?

37. What is the symbol you can use to multiply two values?

38. What is the symbol you can use to subtract two values?

39. What is the symbol you can use to divide two values?

40. What cells am I referencing if I write =SUM(A1:B3)?

41. What cells am I referencing if I write =SUM(A1,B3)?

42. What cells am I referencing if I write =SUM(A:B)?

43. What cells am I referencing if I write =SUM(1:3)?

44. If you just want to know what the sum of a range of cells is but don't need to record that value anywhere, what is one option you have for seeing that sum?

45. How can you see what cells are being used in a formula?

46. What does AutoSum do?

47. Where can you find the AutoSum option?

48. What is one thing to be careful about when using AutoSum?

49. If you want to subtract the values in Cells B1, C1, and D1 from the value in Cell A1, what's the best way to do that?

50. How can you get Excel to help you write your formulas?

51. Is it possible to use Excel to conduct complex calculations in one cell?

52. How do you find a function that can do what you want to do?

53. What does it mean that formulas in Excel are relative?

54. Why is it good that formulas in Excel are relative?

55. What if you want to keep a reference fixed when you copy a formula? For example, Cell A1 includes the unit price and you want that fixed no matter where you copy the formula to?

56. What if you just want to move a formula but you don't want any of the cell references to change. How would you do that?

PRINTING QUIZ

1. What is the control shortcut for printing?

2. How else can you access the print option?

3. If you're ready to print and don't need to make any changes, what button do you click on to print?

4. If you want to print on both sides of the page, which option should you change?

5. When is it best to use print on both sides long-edge versus print on both sides short-edge?

6. What does it mean to print a document collated versus uncollated?

7. What does Print Selection do?

8. What does Print Active Sheets do?

9. What does Print Entire Workbook do?

10. What does Print Selected Pages do?

11. How do you change the printer you're using to print?

12. How do you specify the number of copies to print?

13. What is the difference between portrait orientation and landscape orientation?

14. How do you choose what type of paper to print on?

15. What should you be careful about when selecting the type of paper to print on?

16. What does the margins setting let you do?

17. What does scaling let you do?

18. What should you be careful about when using page scaling?

19. What's one trick for working with scaling if the data isn't going to fit well on the page?

20. Where can you go to scale your document?

21. Where can you go to center your print output horizontally and/or vertically on the page?

22. What does setting a Print Area on a document do?

23. When is setting the Print Area useful?

24. What are the dangers of using Print Area?

25. What's the best way to set the Print Area?

26. What does Print Titles allow you to do?

27. How do you set Print Titles?

28. What should you be careful of when using Print Titles?

CONCLUSION QUIZ

1. Name three ways to find more information if you get stuck.

2. What else can you do if you get stuck?

QUIZ ANSWERS

TERMINOLOGY QUIZ ANSWERS

1. In an Excel worksheet what are generally identified by letters that run across the top of the worksheet?

a. Columns

2. In an Excel worksheet what are generally identified by numbers that run along the left-hand side of the worksheet?

b. Rows

3. What is a cell?

A combination of a row and column that is identified by the letter of the column it's in and the number of the row it's in.

4. How do you know what cell or cell(s) you have selected?

The cell or cells will have a darker border around them. When you've selected cells that are not touching the most recently selected cell will be surrounded by a darker border and the other cells will be shaded in gray.

5. In general, what does left-clicking do?

It selects the item.

6. In general, what does right-clicking do?

It shows a dropdown list of options to choose from.

7. What is the difference between a worksheet and a workbook in Excel?

A worksheet is just one tab that contains a combination of rows and columns within an Excel workbook. A workbook is an entire Excel file. There can be more than one worksheet in an Excel workbook. Worksheets are initially labeled Sheet1, Sheet2, etc.

8. What is the formula bar?

The formula bar is the bar at the top of the screen when you're in Excel with the fx symbol next to it. If you start to type text into a cell, the formula bar will also show what you type. If you input a formula into a cell and then hit enter and go back to that cell, the value returned by the formula will show in the cell, while the formula bar will show the formula being used.

9. What is a scroll bar?

A scroll bar is a bar at the side or bottom of the screen that you can use to navigate through an Excel worksheet.

10. How can you use a scroll bar?

d. All of the above. (Click on the bar and drag, click on the space to either side of the bar, and click on the arrows at the top and bottom or on each end of the scroll bar space.)

11. With a scroll bar if you want to move outside of the area where you've already entered information, which method should you use?

Use the arrows at the ends of the scroll bar.

12. Name two ways that you can select cells in a worksheet.

Left-click and drag your mouse to highlight cells that are touching. Or, left-click on the first cell, hold down the Ctrl key, and then left-click on any other cells you want to select.

13. What is a dropdown menu?

It's a list of potential choices that you can select from, generally indicated by the existence of a small arrow next to the visible choice for that item. See, for example, the list of fonts under the Font section of the Home tab.

14. What is a dialogue box?

It's a pop-up menu of choices for a given task. Generally, dialogue boxes will contain the most choices for a task whereas the information in the tabs contains the most frequently used options.

15. How can you access a dialogue box?

Often they are available when you see a small arrow in the bottom right corner of a section of a tab. See, for example, the Font section of the Home tab.

ABSOLUTE BASICS QUIZ ANSWERS

1. What is the Ctrl shortcut you can use to save a file?
Ctrl + S

2. Which of the following methods works to open an existing Excel file:
d. All of the above. (Double-click on the file name where it's stored on your computer, open Excel and choose the file name from the list under Recent on the left-hand side or navigate to the file location by clicking on Open Other Workbooks at the bottom of the page, or if you're already in Excel, go to File and then choose Open from the left-hand side menu and then choose a file name from under Recent Workbooks or navigate to the file you want using the Computer option.)

3. What is the difference between Save and Save As?
Save will save the file using its existing name, location, and file type and will overwrite the prior version of the file. Save As allows you to change the file name, location, or file type and, if you do so, will not overwrite the prior version of the file. For new files, Excel always defaults to Save As.

4. Discuss why you might save a file as an .xls file type instead of an .xlsx file type.

An .xls file type should be one that anyone with any version of Excel can open. With an .xlsx file type only those who have Excel 2007 or later can open it. So if you're going to share the file and aren't sure what version of Excel the other person is working with, it's better to use the .xls file type, assuming you haven't used any functions that weren't available in prior versions of Excel.

5. Name three ways to save a file.

Ctrl + S, File>Save, click on the image of a computer disk in the top left corner of your screen.

6. How can you delete an existing Excel file?

By navigating to where you have the file saved and deleting it from there. You can either click on the file and then choose Delete from the menu at the top of the box or you can right-click and choose Delete from the dropdown menu.

7. How can you rename an existing Excel file?

You can either choose to Save As and rename the file that way but it will leave you with two versions of the file, one under the old name, one under the new name. Or you can navigate to where the file is saved, click on the file name once to select it, once more to highlight the name, and then type in your new name there.

8. What issue should you be aware of if you move or rename an Excel file that you recently used?

You won't be able to open the file from the list of Recent Workbooks in Excel since the file was moved or renamed and the path that Excel has for it is no longer accurate. You will either need to go to where the file is stored and open it from there or navigate to the file using the Computer option under Open.

NAVIGATING EXCEL QUIZ ANSWERS

1. When you open a new Excel file, what cell and worksheet does it open to?

Cell A1 of Sheet1.

2. When you open an existing Excel file, what cell and worksheet does it open to?

Wherever you were when you last saved the file. This means that it may open with a set of cells already selected.

3. Name two ways you could use to get to Cell B6 if you were in Cell A1?

Left-click on Cell B6. Use the arrow keys to navigate from Cell A1 to Cell B6.

4. What does the Shift key do? What does Shift + Tab do?

The shift key lets you move one cell to the right. Using shift + tab lets you move one cell to the left.

5. In a worksheet that has a lot of data in it, what is a quick way to scroll down a large number of rows or to scroll over a large number of columns?

Click and hold the scroll bar as you drag it either down or over.

6. What is one very important thing you need to remember when using scrollbars to navigate an Excel worksheet?

Until you click into a new cell in the worksheet you will still be in the last cell you clicked on or edited. This means you can scroll down thousands of rows in a worksheet, but if you forget to click into one of the now-visible cells, when you use your arrow key or start typing you will be doing so in the cell thousands of rows away from where you scrolled to.

7. Name two ways to move to a different worksheet than the one you're currently in.

Left-click on the name of the worksheet you want to move to. Or use Ctrl + Page Up to move one worksheet to the left or Ctrl + Page Dn to move one worksheet at a time to the right. (If you're on a computer where the arrow keys and the Page Up/Page Dn keys have been combined you may actually need to use Ctrl + Fn + Page Up and Ctrl + Fn +Page Dn.)

8. What does using the F2 key do?

It takes you to the end of the contents of the current cell. It can be very useful when you need to edit the contents of a cell and don't want to switch to using your mouse or trackpad.

9. Name two ways to insert a cell into a worksheet.

Click in the cell where you want to insert a cell and then right-click and choose Insert from the dropdown menu. Or click in the cell where you want to insert a cell and then go to the Cells section of the Home tab and choose Insert Cells from the Insert dropdown menu.

10. What do the different insert cell options (shift cells right, shift cells down, entire row, and entire column) do?

Shift cells right will insert a cell (or cells) by shifting the selected cell or cells to the right. Shift cells down will insert a cell (or cells) by shifting the selected cell or cells down. Entire row will insert one entire row for each row in the selected range of cells. Entire column will insert one entire column for each column in the selected range of cells.

11. Name three ways you can insert a row or column into a worksheet.

You can select a cell, right click, choose Insert, and then choose Entire Row to insert a row or Entire Column to insert a column. You can also highlight the entire row or column, right-click, and select Insert. Or you can highlight the row or column and then go to the Cells section of the Home tab and choose the option you want from the Insert dropdown menu.

12. How do you select an entire row or column?

Click on the letter of the column or the number of the row.

13. How do you insert a new worksheet into an Excel workbook?

Click on + symbol in a circle (or in older versions of Excel the mini worksheet with a yellow star in the corner) that is at the end of the list of your existing worksheets. Or go to the Home tab and under the Cells section and choose Insert Sheet from the Insert dropdown menu.

14. How do you delete a cell in a worksheet?

Right-click on the cell you want to delete and choose Delete from the dropdown menu. From there choose whether to shift cells up or left to replace the deleted cell. You can also select the cell and then go to the Cells section of the Home tab and click on the Delete dropdown menu and choose Delete Cells from there.

15. What is the problem you might run into when you either insert a cell or cells or delete a cell or cells from a worksheet that has existing data?

You can inadvertently change the alignment of your remaining data so that the data no longer matches up. To avoid this issue, you may sometimes need to insert or delete more cells to keep all of your existing data aligned.

16. How do you delete a column or row?

Highlight the entire column or row you want to delete, right-click, and choose Delete from the dropdown menu. Or you can highlight the column or row, go to the Cells section of the Home tab, and choose the option from the Delete dropdown menu.

17. How do you delete a worksheet?

Right-click on the worksheet name and choose Delete. You can also go to the Cells section of the Home tab and use the Delete Sheet option from the Delete dropdown menu.

18. How do you rename a worksheet?

Double left-click on the worksheet name and then delete the existing name and replace it with the name you want. You can also right-click on the worksheet name and choose Rename from the dropdown menu.

INPUTTING YOUR DATA
QUIZ ANSWERS

1. What is the most basic way to input data in a cell in an Excel worksheet?

Click and start typing.

2. Which of the following are bad ways of inputting data in an Excel worksheet?

e. All of the above. (Not labeling each column of your data, breaking up your data entries with summary entries, allowing users to enter data in any way and any format they want, using a lot of free text entry fields.)

3. What is a best practice when handling a data set that you need to analyze?

Store the raw data in one location, analyze and correct that data in a separate location.

4. What does Ctrl + Z do?

It undoes the last thing you did in Excel.

5. What does Ctrl + Y do?

It redoes the last thing you did in Excel.

6. If you have to make a large number of entries in a column in Excel that have a limited number of values (say, book, CD, and video), what's an easy trick for entering that information that will save you a lot of time?

You can use the Excel auto-suggested text feature to make your entries. As long as the entries all start with a different letter, you've already entered each one at least once, and your entries are continuous, when you type the first letter of each entry Excel will suggest to you that word that you already used and you can just hit enter to have Excel populate that cell with the entire word even though you only typed the first letter.

7. Does auto-suggested text work with numbers?

No. It only works with entries that have letters in them. It will work with something like 123alpha but only when you type 123a. Until then it won't work.

8. Name two ways to copy the contents of a cell.

Click on the cell and type Ctrl + C. Right-click on the cell and choose Copy from the dropdown menu. (You can also use the Copy option in the Clipboard section of the Home tab.)

9. Name two ways to cut the contents of a cell from its current location.

Click on the cell and type Ctrl + X. Right-click on the cell and choose Cut from the dropdown menu. (You can also use the Cut option in the Clipboard section of the Home tab.)

10. Name two ways to paste the contents of a cell into a new location.

After you've copied or cut the contents of a cell, you can go to the new location, click into the cell where you want the information and hit enter. You can also use Ctrl

+ V at the new location. The advantage of using Ctrl + V is that it allows you to paste those values into more than one location as long as the information was copied not cut from its prior location. (You can also use the Paste option in the Clipboard section of the Home tab.)

11. When it comes to formulas, what is the difference between Copying the contents of a cell and Cutting the contents of a cell?

If you Cut the contents of a cell and place them in a new location, the formula remains exactly the same as it was. So =A1+B1 will still be =A1+B1. If you Copy the contents of a cell and place them in a new location, the formula will adjust relative to its new location. So if you move a formula that was =A1+B1 down two rows it will become =A3+B3. If you move it over two columns instead it will become =C1+D1.

12. What does using the $ sign in a formula do?

It fixes the row or column reference so that if the formula is copied to another cell, the row or column reference will stay the same. For example, if the formula was =$A1+B$1, meaning keep the Column A reference in A1 fixed and the Row 1 reference in B1 fixed, then if that formula is copied down two rows, the formula would now be =$A3+B$1. And if it was copied over two columns instead it would be =$A1+D$1. Using the dollar sign for both the row and column, so for example $A$1, means that the reference to that particular cell will remain the same no matter where the formula is copied.

13. What does Paste Special – Values do?

It allows you to paste copied entries and only retain the values of any calculations from the copied cells without also copying the formulas or formatting. This also lets you paste in values but use the formatting of the destination cells instead of the originating cells.

14. What does Paste Special – Transpose do?

It allows you to copy a row of values and paste them as a column of values or to copy a column of values and paste them as a row. Be careful with this one that you don't overwrite existing data.

15. How can you display the contents of a cell as text without Excel trying to convert it into a date or formula?

Use a single quotation mark to start your entry. For example '-Item A will display as –Item A but not using the single quotation mark will have Excel trying to treat that as a formula.

16. How do you tell Excel that you're entering a formula into a cell?

By starting the entry with a -, +, or = sign. It's best to use the = sign if you can.

17. How can you include line breaks within a cell in Excel (since hitting enter will just take you to the next cell)?

By using Alt + Enter.

18. How can you delete data you've entered into a cell without deleting the cell?

Click in the cell and use your delete key to remove the contents. You can also use F2 or double-click to get into the cell and then use the backspace key. To delete the contents of a cell as well as the formatting on the cell, go to the Editing section of the Home tab and choose Clear All from the Clear dropdown menu.

19. What does Find do?

It allows you to find an entry that matches your criteria.

20. What does Replace do?

It allows you to find an entry that matches your criteria and replace it with another value.

21. What is the danger of using Replace?

If you're not careful in specifying what you wanted to find, you can end up replacing part of an entry you didn't intend to replace. For example, if you try to replace "hat" with "chapeau" and are not specific that you're only looking for the full word hat, you can end up replacing all occurrences of hat with chapeau even if they are part of words like that and chat.

22. How do you access Find and Replace?

To access Find and Replace you can use Ctrl +F or Ctrl + H to bring up the Find and Replace dialogue box. There's one tab for each option. Or you can go to the Editing section of the Home tab, click on Find & Select and then choose Find or Replace from the dropdown menu there.

23. If you want to have a list of 250 entries that repeat the days of the week (Monday, Tuesday, Wednesday, etc.) what is the easiest way to do that?

Start with Monday in the first cell and then left-click in the bottom right corner and drag until you have the number of entries you want. Excel should auto-complete the rest of the entries Monday, Tuesday, Wednesday, Thursday, Friday, Saturday, Sunday, Monday, etc. (If that doesn't work, fill in the first four cells or so and then try it.)

24. What does Freeze Panes do?

It allows you to specify rows at the top of the worksheet and/or columns at the left-hand side of the worksheet that you want to keep always visible.

25. How do you Freeze Panes?

Go to the View tab and choose Freeze Panes from the

Window section. From there choose whether you want to Freeze Top Row, Freeze First Column, or Freeze Panes. Freeze Panes will freeze all of the columns to the left of the cell you're clicked into and all of the rows above the cell you're clicked into.

26. What is one thing to be careful of when using Freeze Panes?

If you're clicked into one of the top rows or side columns that you've frozen and you arrow down or over to an area that isn't frozen you can lose your place, because arrowing down or over will take you to the next row or column not necessarily the rows or columns that are visible to you at that moment.

Also, if you freeze too many panes you won't be able to see any of your other data.

FORMATTING QUIZ ANSWERS

1. What are the Ctrl shortcuts for bolding, italics, and underlining?

Ctrl + B to bold, Ctrl + I to italicize, and Ctrl + U to underline.

2. What are the six basic cell alignment choices you have available to you?

Left, Center, Right, Top, Middle, Bottom

3. How do you align text within a cell?

Click on the cell, go to the Alignment section of the Home tab, and choose and click on the cell alignment option that you want to use. The images on the buttons show each alignment type. Another option is to right-click on the cell and choose Format Cells from the dropdown menu. From there go to the Alignment tab and change the Horizontal and Vertical dropdown options to what you want.

4. If you want to change the angle of text, how do you do that?

One option is to click on the cell and then go to the Alignment section of the Home tab and choose from one of the options under the Orientation dropdown (the ab with an angled arrow under it on the top row). Another option is to right-click, choose Format Cells from the dropdown menu, go to the Alignment tab, and then in the Orientation section on the right-hand side choose the degree to which you want to angle your text.

5. What are two other ways to bold text other than using a Ctrl shortcut?

Click on the large capital B in the Font section of the Home tab. Right-click, choose Format Cells from the dropdown menu, go to the Font tab, and choose Bold for your Font Style.

6. What are two other ways to italicize text other than using a Ctrl shortcut?

Click on the slanted capital I in the Font section of the Home tab. Right-click, choose Format Cells from the dropdown menu, go to the Font tab, and choose Italic for your Font Style.

7. What are two other ways to underline text other than using a Ctrl shortcut?

Click on the underlined capital U in the Font section of the Home tab. Right-click, choose Format Cells from the dropdown menu, go to the Font tab, and choose an option from the Underline dropdown menu.

8. If you have selected text that is partially formatted in bold, italic, or underline and partially not, what will happen when you click on the B, I, or U for bold, italic, or underline formatting?

It will apply that formatting to the entire selection. Which means to remove that type of formatting from a selection that is partially formatted that way you will need to click on the option twice, once to apply the formatting to the entire selection, once to remove it.

9. When should you choose the style of border that you want to use for a given cell?

Before you apply that border to that cell. If you don't, the border applied to the cell will be the default or current border format you have selected.

10. How can you put a diagonal border line through a cell?

Highlight the cell, right-click, choose Format Cells, go to the Border tab and click on the diagonal option in the bottom corner under the Border section.

11. Name two ways to apply a standard border to a cell.

Use the Border dropdown option in the Font section of the Home tab. Or right-click on the cell, choose Format Cells, go to the Border tab, and click on the border option there.

12. If you just want a simple border around all of your cells, what's the best border option to use?

All Borders.

13. To put a darker perimeter border around a range of cells, what default option can you choose?

Thick Box Border.

14. How do you clear all borders from around a cell or cells?

Highlight the cells and then choose the No Border option from the dropdown or the None border option in the Format Cells dialogue box.

15. How do you add background color to a cell?

Use Fill Color which can be most easily accessed from the Font section of the Home tab by clicking on the paint bucket that by default has a yellow line under it.

16. If you need to use a custom fill color or custom font color, how do you do this?

Click on the fill color or font color dropdown to bring up the colors dropdown menu. At the bottom of the menu click on the More Colors option to bring up the Colors dialogue box. Go to the Custom tab and provide your RGB or HSL values.

17. Name three ways to adjust the width of a column.

Right-click on the column and choose Column Width from the dropdown menu and then input a value. Place your cursor to the right side of the column and then left-click and hold while dragging the column to the desired width. Or place your cursor on the right side of the column and double-left click to get the column to auto-adjust to the contents in the column.

18. How can you adjust all of your column widths at once?

Select all cells in the worksheet and then either double-left click on any column to get the columns to adjust to their contents or left-click and drag on one column's border line to change all column widths to the same new column width. If you need a specific column width you can also select all cells in the worksheet and then right-click on a column and choose Column Width to specify the needed column width.

19. How do you select all cells in a worksheet?

Click in the top left corner between the label for Column A and Row 1. Or use Ctrl + A.

20. Name three ways to adjust the height of a row.

Right-click on the row and choose Row Height from the dropdown menu and then input a value. Place your cursor at the bottom of the row and then left-click and hold while dragging the row to the desired height. Or place your cursor on the bottom of the row and double-left click to get the row to auto-adjust to the contents in the column.

21. How can you adjust all of your row heights at once?

Select all cells in the worksheet and then either double-left click on any row to get the rows to adjust to their contents or left-click and drag on any row border line to change all row heights to the same new row height. If you need a specific row height you can also select all cells in the worksheet and then right-click on a row and choose Row Height to specify the needed row height.

22. How do you get text to wrap to the next line?

Use Wrap Text which is available under the Alignment section of the Home tab. It's also available by right-clicking, choosing Format Cells, going to the Alignment tab, and selecting the Wrap Text option.

23. Name three ways you can apply currency formatting to a cell or range of cells.

Click on the $ sign in the Number section of the Home tab. Go to the Number section of the Home tab and choose Accounting or Currency from the dropdown menu. Right-click and choose Format Cells from the dropdown menu and then go to the Number tab and choose either Currency or Accounting from there.

24. Name two ways you can apply date formatting to a cell or range of cells.

Go to the Number section of the Home tab and choose the Short Date or Long Date option from the dropdown menu. Or right-click, choose Format Cells from the dropdown menu, go to the Number tab and choose Date for the category and then a date format from one of the available samples.

25. What is one thing to be careful of when using dates in Excel?

You need to be aware that Excel will always assign a year to a date even if you don't. So if you type in Jan-1, Excel will make that date into January 1st of the current year.

26. Name two ways you can change the font used in a cell or range of cells.

Go to the Font section of the Home tab and choose a different font from the font dropdown box. Right click, choose Format Cells from the dropdown menu, go to the Font tab, and choose your Font from the available list of fonts.

27. Name four ways to change the size of the font used in a cell or range of cells.

Go to the Font section of the Home tab and choose a different font size from the font size dropdown menu. Go to the Font section of the Home tab and type in a new font size where the current font size is displayed. Go to the Font section of the Home tab and use the Increase Font Size and Decrease Font Size options. Right-click, choose Format Cells, go to the Font tab and choose a new font size from the listed values or type in a new value.

28. How do you change the color of the text in a cell or range of cells?

Go to the Font section of the Home tab and click on the Font Color dropdown, which is the A with a red line under it by default, and then choose the color you want from the listed options or by clicking on More Colors. Or you can right-click, choose to Format Cells, go to the Font tab, and click on the dropdown menu under Color and choose a color from there.

29. If you've placed a dark fill color into a cell, what font color might you want to use?

White or another light color that will show over a dark color.

30. What does Merge & Center do?

It merges multiple cells into one cell and centers any text that was in the top left cell of the range across the newly-created single cell.

31. When might you want to use Merge & Center?

When creating a table of data where you want a single cell that runs across the top that labels a range of cells below that.

32. How do you Merge & Center a range of cells?

Highlight the cells you want to merge, go to the Alignment section of the Home tab and choose Merge & Center. You can also highlight the cells, right-click, choose Format Cells from the dropdown menu, go to the Alignment tab, and then choose Merge Cells from there. With this option you'll have to center the text separately.

33. If you want to format a range of cells as a number with four decimal places, how would you do that?

Highlight the cells and then go to the Number section of the Home tab and choose the Number option from the dropdown menu. This will create a number with two decimal places. Next, click on the Increase Decimal option twice to add two more decimal places. Or you can highlight the cells, right-click, choose Format Cells, go to the Number tab, choose Number on the left-hand side, and then in the middle specify the number of decimal places you need.

34. How do you format a number as a percentage?

You can click on the percent sign in the Number section of the Home tab or you can right-click, choose Format Cells, go to the Number tab, and choose Percentage from there.

35. If you have the number .10 what is that as a percentage?

10%

36. What does the Format Painter allow you to do?

It allows you to copy the formatting from one cell or a range of cells to another cell or range of cells.

37. How do you use the Format Painter?

Click on the selection that has the formatting you want, then click on the Format Painter tool under the Clipboard section of the Home tab, then highlight the cell or cells where you want to apply that formatting.

38. What would happen if you click on the Format Painter tool and then try to use the arrow keys to navigate to the cell where you want to apply that formatting?

You'd end up applying that formatting to the first cell you arrow to.

39. How can you apply formatting to multiple cells that are not touching without having to go through the whole Format Painter process each time?

Click on the selection that has the formatting you want, *double-click* on the Format Painter tool, and then click on all of the cells you want to have that formatting before clicking on the Format Painter tool again to turn it off.

MANIPULATING YOUR DATA
QUIZ ANSWERS

1. What does Sorting do?

It allows you to take a range of cells and sort them based upon criteria you specify. For example, by date and then customer name and then amount spent.

2. Do you need to have a header row to sort data?

No.

3. If your data does have a header row, what do you need to make sure you do when you are telling Excel how to sort your data?

Make sure "my data has headers" is selected in the top right corner of the Sort dialogue box.

4. What will happen if your data has a header row but Excel doesn't know that?

Excel will sort the header row as if it's any other row of data.

5. Should you include a summary row in your sort?

No. Because Excel will treat that summary row as any other row of data and will sort it that way.

6. Name three ways to sort a range of data.

Select the cells you want to sort, go to the Editing section of the Home tab, click on the Sort & Filter dropdown, and choose Custom Sort. You can also go to the Data tab and click on the Sort option there. Or you can right-click and choose Sort and then Custom Sort from the dropdown menu.

7. If the sort options that you see are Column A, Column B, Column C, etc. what does this mean?

That Excel doesn't think that your data has a header row.

8. What order should you list your sort criteria in?

From the first one you want used to the last one you want used. So if you want to sort by date and then name, be sure to list date as your first sort criteria and name second.

9. If you want to sort text in an alphabetical order, which sort options should you choose?

Values and A to Z.

10. If you want to sort numbers from largest to smallest, which sort options should you choose?

Values and Largest to Smallest.

11. If you have a range that contains days of the week or months of the year, what sort options should you choose?

Values, Custom List, and then the list that corresponds to how you've written the days of the week or months of the year.

12. If you added a sort level that you don't need, how do you remove it?

Click on that level and then choose Delete Level.

13. How do you change the order in which your data will be sorted when you have multiple sort criteria listed?

Click on a level you want to move and then use the up and down arrows at the top of the Sort dialogue box to move your sort criteria into the desired order.

14. What are some issues to be aware of when sorting?

Be sure that you've selected all related data before you sort. If you only select one column of data and sort it, the data in other columns will not sort and that can lead to a mismatch in your data entries. (Another reason to always keep your raw data stored in one location and to manipulate that data elsewhere.)

That if you have a header column and don't tell Excel that it's a header column it will be included in the sort just like any other row. Same with any summary row.

15. What should you do if you sort data and realize you made a mistake?

Ctrl + Z to Undo the sort and try again.

16. What does filtering do?

It allows you to take a set of data and apply filters to that data so that only certain results are displayed. The underlying data remains in the same order as before.

17. How do you turn on filtering?

Click into a cell in the header row of your data and then go to the Editing section of the Home tab, click on the arrow next to Sort & Filter, and choose Filter.

18. If you add a new column of data, will filtering extend to that new column?

No. You will need to turn off filtering and then turn it back on to include the new column.

19. How will you know when you have filtering turned on?

You'll see small gray arrows in the bottom right corner of the header row for each column that has filtering available.

20. Once you've turned on filtering, how do you filter a specific column?

Click on the gray arrow in the header row for that column and then choose your filter criteria.

21. In recent versions of Excel, what options do you have for filtering data?

You can specify text, you can click on the box to select specific entries, you can use text or number filters, and you can filter by cell or font color.

22. Using filtering, if you just want to see two or three specific entries in a column but have a large number of different values that are possible in that column, what's a quick trick to do that?

Click on the Select All option to unselect all of the entries and then just click on the two or three entries you want to see.

23. Using filtering, if you want to see all of the entries that contain the word "USA", how would you do that?

Use the Search option and type in USA.

24. Using filtering, if you want to see all of the entries that have red text, how would you do that?

Use the Filter by Color option, choose Filter by Font Color, and then click on the red option.

25. Using filtering, if you want to see all of the entries with a numerical value greater than 100, how would you do that?

Use the Number Filters option, choose Greater Than, and then specify 100 as your value.

26. How can you tell when your worksheet values have already been filtered?

The row numbers in your worksheet will be colored blue and you'll see that the row numbers skip values.

27. How can you tell which columns have filtering in place?

The gray arrow will turn into a funnel.

28. How do you remove filtering from a specific column?

Click on the funnel and choose Clear Filter from [Column Name].

29. How do you remove filtering from all columns in a worksheet?

Go to the Editing section of the Home tab, click on Sort & Filter, and then choose Clear.

30. How do you turn off filtering?

Go to the Editing section of the Home tab, click on Sort & Filter, and click on Filter.

31. How do you tell Excel that you want to use a function?

Start your entry with an = sign.

32. What is the function you can use to sum a range of values?

SUM

33. What is the function you can use to multiply a range of values?

PRODUCT

34. Is there a function for subtracting values?
No.

35. Is there a function for dividing values?
No.

36. What is the symbol you can use to add two values?
The + symbol.

37. What is the symbol you can use to multiply two values?
The * symbol.

38. What is the symbol you can use to subtract two values?
The - symbol.

39. What is the symbol you can use to divide two values?
The / symbol

40. What cells am I referencing if I write =SUM(A1:B3)?
Cells A1, B1, A2, B2, A3, and B3

41. What cells am I referencing if I write =SUM(A1,B3)?
Cells A1 and B3

42. What cells am I referencing if I write =SUM(A:B)?
All the cells in Columns A and B

43. What cells am I referencing if I write =SUM(1:3)?
All the cells in Rows 1, 2, and 3

44. If you just want to know what the sum of a range of cells is but don't need to record that value anywhere, what is one option you have for seeing that sum?

You can simply select the cells and then look in the bottom right corner of the Excel worksheet where it shows the SUM for the selected cells.

45. How can you see what cells are being used in a formula?

Double-click into the cell where the formula is and Excel will highlight all of the cells being used in the formula in a color that matches the cell reference within the formula that you're reviewing.

46. What does AutoSum do?

It allows you to sum a range of values by clicking in the cell at the end of that range of values and choosing the AutoSum option. Excel will then write the sum formula for you.

47. Where can you find the AutoSum option?

In the Editing section of the Home tab.

48. What is one thing to be careful about when using AutoSum?

If there are gaps in the range of values you want to sum, the AutoSum function will not sum the entire range of values, but will instead stop at the first gap in your data.

49. If you want to subtract the values in Cells B1, C1, and D1 from the value in Cell A1, what's the best way to do that?

Use the formula =A1-SUM(B1:D1)

(Writing =A1-B1-C1-D1 would also work, but is not the best way to do it.)

50. How can you get Excel to help you write your formulas?

Once you start a function or formula, Excel will populate any cells that you highlight into the function or formula. So you can type =SUM(and then go highlight the range of values you want to sum and Excel will translate those highlight cells into cell notation for you. This is especially helpful when you're using cell references across worksheets.

51. Is it possible to use Excel to conduct complex calculations in one cell?

Yes, but be careful about where you place your parens to make sure that the calculations are performed in the correct order.

52. How do you find a function that can do what you want to do?

Go to the Formulas tab and click on Insert Function to bring up the Insert Function dialogue box. You can then search in the "search for a function" box and then click on the functions Excel lists to see a description of what each one does and how to write it.

53. What does it mean that formulas in Excel are relative?

It means that when you copy a formula to a new cell it will adjust all of the cell references based on how far the formula was moved. So A1+B1 becomes C1+D1 if that formula is copied over two columns and becomes A3+B3 if it's copied down two rows.

54. Why is it good that formulas in Excel are relative?

Because this allows you to write a formula once and then copy it to a large number of cells without having to rewrite it each time. For example, if you're calculating amount owed from your customers based upon how many units of your product they bought you can write a formula that multiplies units times price and then just copy that down all the customer rows. As long as units and price are in the same relative location for each customer, you only have to write the formula that one time.

55. What if you want to keep a reference fixed when you copy a formula? For example, Cell A1 includes the unit price and you want that fixed no matter where you copy the formula to?

Then use the $ sign to fix your cell reference. If you want to always be referencing Cell A1 than the formula should use $A$1.

56. What if you just want to move a formula but you don't want any of the cell references to change. How would you do that?

Then cut that formula (Ctrl + X) instead of copying the formula (Ctrl + C). You can also click into the cell, copy the text of the formula, go to the new location, and paste the text in that way.

PRINTING
QUIZ ANSWERS

1. What is the control shortcut for printing?
Ctrl + P

2. How else can you access the print option?
Go to the File tab and select Print.

3. If you're ready to print and don't need to make any changes, what button do you click on to print?
The printer icon labeled print.

4. If you want to print on both sides of the page, which option should you change?
The one that by default is labeled print one sided.

5. When is it best to use print on both sides long-edge versus print on both sides short-edge?
It's best to print on both sides long-edge when your document has a portrait orientation and to use print on both sides short-edge when your document has a landscape orientation.

6. What does it mean to print a document collated versus uncollated?

This only matters when there are multiple pages to the document and you're printing more than one copy. If you print collated all pages for each copy will print at once. If you print uncollated the first page will print for as many copies as you specified and then the second page will print and so on.

7. What does Print Selection do?

It prints only the cells you've highlighted in your Excel workbook. (This can mean that you print across worksheets if you happened to have multiple worksheets selected when you highlighted your cells.)

8. What does Print Active Sheets do?

It prints all of the worksheets that you've selected. You can select multiple worksheets by using the Ctrl key as you click on each one.

9. What does Print Entire Workbook do?

It prints all worksheets in your Excel file.

10. What does Print Selected Pages do?

It allows you to only print certain pages from your selected worksheet(s). You can use the Print Preview to see what information is available on each page.

11. How do you change the printer you're using to print?

Select a new printer from the dropdown menu under Printer at the top of the screen.

12. How do you specify the number of copies to print?

Change the number where it says Copies at the top of the screen. You can either use the arrows or type in a new value.

13. What is the difference between portrait orientation and landscape orientation?

Portrait orientation has the longer edge of the page along the side and the shorter edge at the top, like most books. Landscape orientation has the long edge at the top and the short edge on the side, like many landscape paintings or PowerPoint presentations.

14. How do you choose what type of paper to print on?

Change the dropdown that by default says Letter to the type of paper you need to print on.

15. What should you be careful about when selecting the type of paper to print on?

Make sure that type of paper is actually available to you to print on.

16. What does the margins setting let you do?

Change the amount of white space that's left available around the edges of the page.

17. What does scaling let you do?

Reduce the overall size of your information so that it fits onto one page or so that all rows or columns fit on one page.

18. What should you be careful about when using page scaling?

That you don't make the information so small that it's no longer legible.

19. What's one trick for working with scaling if the data isn't going to fit well on the page?

Change your document orientation to landscape so that more columns can fit on the page without reducing the size of the font as much.

20. Where can you go to scale your document?

If you just want to fit everything on one page or all columns or rows on one page those options are available on the main print screen under the dropdown that by default says No Scaling. But if you want to scale across a specified number of pages, then you can click on Page Setup and go to the Page tab and then specify your number of pages wide and tall.

21. Where can you go to center your print output horizontally and/or vertically on the page?

Click on Page Setup and then go to the Margins tab and click the option you want.

22. What does setting a Print Area on a document do?

It limits the area of that document that will be printed to just the selected range of cells.

23. When is setting the Print Area useful?

When you have a number of calculations or notes on a worksheet, but only ever want to print a small section of that worksheet.

24. What are the dangers of using Print Area?

If you add more information to the worksheet but forget that you've set a print area, you may not understand why the new data isn't printing.

25. What's the best way to set the Print Area?

While you're in the active worksheet, highlight the cells you want to print, go to the Page Layout tab, and click on the Print Area dropdown, and choose Set Print Area from there.

26. What does Print Titles allow you to do?

It allows you to specify a row or rows and a column or columns that will print on every single page of your document. This is great when you have a large set of data that can't be printed on one page and need a header row or column with identifiers visible on each page.

27. How do you set Print Titles?

While in your active worksheet go to the Page Layout tab and click on Print Titles. This will bring up the Sheet tab of the Page Setup dialogue box. Click in the box for rows to repeat at the top and then select the rows you want to have repeat from your worksheet. Next, click on the box for columns to repeat at left and select the columns you want to repeat.

28. What should you be careful of when using Print Titles?

If you tell Excel to repeat too many rows at the top or too many columns on the side you can end up just printing those rows and columns over and over again without printing the rest of the data in the worksheet.

CONCLUSION QUIZ ANSWERS

1. Name three ways to find more information if you get stuck.

Click on the ? mark in the top right corner of your Excel workbook and search for information on the topic. Click on the Tell Me More option available under certain menu items, such as Format Painter. Do an internet search on your topic and look for the www.support.office.com search result.

2. What else can you do if you get stuck?

Search for forums where someone else has already asked your question. Or email me at mlhumphreywriter@gmail.com.

BONUS: EXERCISES

EXERCISE 1

Recreate the following image where the total value in Column E is calculated by multiplying the units times the price for each customer.

	A	B	C	D	E
1	Date	Customer Name	Units	Price	Total
2	1/1/2018	Bob Jones	10	$2.50	$25.00
3	3/4/2018	Albert Cross	15	$2.50	$37.50
4	5/1/2018	Bob Jones	10	$2.50	$25.00
5	6/1/2018	Albert Cross	20	$2.50	$50.00

EXERCISE 2

Recreate the following image where the values in Cells I5 and K5 sum the values in the three rows above those cells:

	H	I	J	K	L
1		**Cash**	**Category**	**CC**	
2		$0.00	**Gas**	$59.73	
3		$13.02	**Misc**	$0.00	
4		$0.00	**Groceries**	$94.21	
5		**$13.02**	**TOTAL**	**$153.94**	
6					

EXERCISE 3

Recreate the following image making sure to use AutoComplete to populate the days of the week and an addition formula to populate the dates in Rows 3 through 8. Also, Column J should be the total of the values in Columns C through I for each row.

	A	B	C	D	E	F	G	H	I	J
1			Monday	Tuesday	Wednesday	Thursday	Friday	Saturday	Sunday	
2	7/3/2017	7/9/2017	0.25	1.5	2.5	3.5	0.5	0	1	9.25
3	7/10/2017	7/16/2017								0
4	7/17/2017	7/23/2017								0
5	7/24/2017	7/30/2017								0
6	7/31/2017	8/6/2017								0
7	8/7/2017	8/13/2017								0
8	8/14/2017	8/20/2017								0
9										

EXERCISE 4

Recreate the following image where the values in Column E are the product of the values in Columns C and D for each row, the values in Column F is the value in Column B divided by Cell B3 for each row, and the values in Column G are the value in Column E times the value in Column F for each row.

	A	B	C	D	E	F	G
1							
2		Amazon Unit Sales	List Price	Payout	Net Per Sale	% Book 1 to This Book	Value of New Customer
3	Book 1	500	$0.99	35%	$0.35	100%	$0.35
4	Book 2	250	$3.99	70%	$2.79	50%	$1.40
5	Book 3	125	$4.99	70%	$3.49	25%	$0.87
6	Book 4	100	$4.99	70%	$3.49	20%	$0.70
7	Book 5	75	$5.99	70%	$4.19	15%	$0.63
8							$3.94

EXERCISE 5

Recreate the following image where the values in Cells C3 through H7 are calculated values using a formula copies from Cell C3 that uses the $ sign to keep the references to Column B and Row 2 fixed. The formula in Cell C3 multiplies the value in Cell C2 by the value in B3.

	A	B	C	D	E	F	G	H
1		Weekly	Hours Worked					
2			10	20	30	40	50	60
3		$8.50	$85.00	$170.00	$255.00	$340.00	$425.00	$510.00
4	Wages	$9.00	$90.00	$180.00	$270.00	$360.00	$450.00	$540.00
5		$9.50	$95.00	$190.00	$285.00	$380.00	$475.00	$570.00
6		$10.00	$100.00	$200.00	$300.00	$400.00	$500.00	$600.00
7		$10.50	$105.00	$210.00	$315.00	$420.00	$525.00	$630.00
8								

BONUS:
EXERCISE ANSWERS

EXERCISE 1

Recreate the following image where the total value in Column E is calculated by multiplying the units times the price for each customer.

	A	B	C	D	E
1	Date	Customer Name	Units	Price	Total
2	1/1/2018	Bob Jones	10	$2.50	$25.00
3	3/4/2018	Albert Cross	15	$2.50	$37.50
4	5/1/2018	Bob Jones	10	$2.50	$25.00
5	6/1/2018	Albert Cross	20	$2.50	$50.00

1. Enter "Date", "Customer Name", "Units", "Price" and "Total" in Cells A1 through E1 respectively.

2. Enter "1/1", "3/4", "5/1" and "6/1 in Cells A2 through A5 respectively. Format as Short Date.

3. Enter "Bob Jones", "Albert Cross", "Bob Jones", and "Albert Cross" into Cells B2 through B5 respectively.

4. Enter "10", "15", "10", and "20" into Cells C2 through

C5 respectively.

5. Enter $2.50 into Cell D2 and format as Currency. Copy down to Cells D3 through D5.

6. Add the formula =C2*D2 to Cell E2 and then copy it down to Cells E3 through E5.

7. Highlight the columns and double-left click on the side of Column B to autosize the column width to the contents.

8. Italicize the dates in Column A.

9. Underline the column headers in Row 1.

10. Place a basic border (All Borders) around Cells A1 through E5.

11. Place a darker outer border (Thick Box Border) around Cells A1 through E5.

EXERCISE 2

Recreate the following image where the values in Cells I5 and K5 sum the values in the three rows above those cells:

	H	I	J	K	L
1		**Cash**	**Category**	**CC**	
2		$0.00	**Gas**	$59.73	
3		$13.02	**Misc**	$0.00	
4		$0.00	**Groceries**	$94.21	
5		**$13.02**	**TOTAL**	**$153.94**	
6					

1. In Cells I1 through I3 type "Cash", "Category", and "CC" respectively.

2. In Cells J2 through J5 type "Gas", "Misc", "Groceries", and "TOTAL" respectively.

3. In Cells I2 through I4 type "0", "13.02", and "0" respectively.

4. In Cells K2 through K4 type "59.73", "0", and "94.21" respectively.

5. In Cell I5 add the formula =SUM(I2:I4).

6. In Cell K5 add the formula =SUM(K2:K4).

7. Bold the values in Cells I1 through K1 and Cells J2 through J5, and in Cells I5 and K5.

8. Format Cells I2 through I5 and K2 through K5 as Currency.

9. Add a fill color to Cells I1 through K1 and J2 through J5.

10. Add a basic border (All Borders) around all of the cells.

11. Center align all of the cells.

EXERCISE 3

Recreate the following image making sure to use AutoComplete to populate the days of the week and an addition formula to populate the dates in Rows 3 through 8. Also, Column J should be the total of the values in Columns C through I for each row.

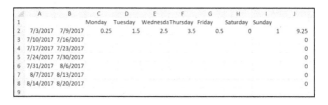

	A	B	C	D	E	F	G	H	I	J
1			Monday	Tuesday	Wednesda	Thursday	Friday	Saturday	Sunday	
2	7/3/2017	7/9/2017	0.25	1.5	2.5	3.5	0.5	0	1	9.25
3	7/10/2017	7/16/2017								0
4	7/17/2017	7/23/2017								0
5	7/24/2017	7/30/2017								0
6	7/31/2017	8/6/2017								0
7	8/7/2017	8/13/2017								0
8	8/14/2017	8/20/2017								0
9										

1. Type "Monday" into Cell C1 and then click and drag from the bottom right corner of the cell over to Cell I1 to populate the rest of the days of the week.

2. Type "7/3/17" and "7/9/17" into Cells A2 and B2 respectively.

3. In Cell A3 add the formula =A2+7.

4. Copy the formula from Cell A3 to Cells A3 through B8. Adjust Column B's width so that all dates are visible.

5. In Cells C2 through I2 add the values "0.25", "1.5", "2.5", "3.5.", "0.5", "0", and "1" respectively.

6. In Cell J2 add the formula =SUM(C2:I2). (You could use AutoSum here as well.)

7. Copy the formula from J2 to Cells J3 through J8.

EXERCISE 4

Recreate the following image where the values in Column E are the product of the values in Columns C and D for each row, the values in Column F is the value in Column B divided by Cell B3 for each row, and the values in Column G are the value in Column E times the value in Column F for each row.

	A	B	C	D	E	F	G
1							
2		Amazon Unit Sales	List Price	Payout	Net Per Sale	% Book 1 to This Book	Value of New Customer
3	Book 1	500	$0.99	35%	$0.35	100%	$0.35
4	Book 2	250	$3.99	70%	$2.79	50%	$1.40
5	Book 3	125	$4.99	70%	$3.49	25%	$0.87
6	Book 4	100	$4.99	70%	$3.49	20%	$0.70
7	Book 5	75	$5.99	70%	$4.19	15%	$0.63
8							$3.94

1. In Cells B2 through G2 add the text "Amazon Unit Sales", "List Price", "Payout", "Net Per Sale", "% Book 1 to This Book", and "Value of New Customer" respectively.

2. In Cells A3 through A7 add "Book 1", "Book 2", "Book3", "Book4" and "Book 5". (You can just add Book 1 and Book 2 and then highlight both cells and click and drag from the bottom right corner of Cell A4 to populate the rest of the values.)

3. Bold the entries in Cells B2 through G2 and A3 through A7. Wrap text for Cells B2 through G2.

4. In Cells B3 through B7 add the values "500", "250", "125", "100" and "75" respectively.

5. In Cells C3 through C7 add the values "0.99", "3.99", "4.99", "4.99", and "5.99" respectively. Format as Currency.

6. In Cells D3 through D4 add the values ".35" and ".7", respectively. Format as a Percentage and then copy the value from Cell D4 to Cells D5 through D7.

7. In Cell E3 add the formula =C3*D3.

8. Copy the value in Cell E3 to Cells E4 through E7.

9. In Cell F3 add the formula =B3/$B$3. Copy the formula from Cell F3 to Cells F4 through F7 and format Cells F3 through F7 as a percentage.

10. In Cell G3 add the formula =E3*F3.

11. Copy the value from G3 to G4 through G7.

12. In Cell G8 use AutoSum to sum the values in Cells G3 through G7. Bold the result. (You can also just use a SUM function =SUM(G3:G7).)

13. Place a basic border (All Borders) around Cells B3 through G7.

EXERCISE 5

Recreate the following image where the values in Cells C3 through H7 are calculated values using a formula copies from Cell C3 that uses the $ sign to keep the references to Column B and Row 2 fixed. The formula in Cell C3 multiplies the value in Cell C2 by the value in B3.

	A	B	C	D	E	F	G	H
1		**Weekly**	**Hours Worked**					
2			10	20	30	40	50	60
3		$8.50	$85.00	$170.00	$255.00	$340.00	$425.00	$510.00
4	Wages	$9.00	$90.00	$180.00	$270.00	$360.00	$450.00	$540.00
5		$9.50	$95.00	$190.00	$285.00	$380.00	$475.00	$570.00
6		$10.00	$100.00	$200.00	$300.00	$400.00	$500.00	$600.00
7		$10.50	$105.00	$210.00	$315.00	$420.00	$525.00	$630.00
8								

1. In Cell B1 type "Weekly" and bold it.

2. In Cell C1 type "Hours Worked" and bold it.

3. Select Cells C1 through H1 and Merge & Center.

4. Add fill color to the newly merged cell that spans Cells C1 through H1.

5. In Cell A3 type "Wages" and bold it.

6. Select Cells A3 through A7 and Merge and Center.

7. Add fill color to the newly merged cell that spans Cells A3 through A7.

8. Change the orientation of the text that spans Cells A3 through A7 to Rotate Text Up and adjust the column width to fit the text. Middle Align the text in the cell.

9. In Cells B3 through B7 add the values "8.50", "9.00", "9.50", "10.00", and "10.50", respectively. (This could also be done with a mathematical formula as well where you input 8.50 and then use =B3+.5 in the next cell and copy that formula down the rest of the way.)

10. In Cells C2 through H2 add the values "10", "20", "30", "40", "50", and "60" respectively. (This could also be done with a mathematical formula where you type 10 into Cells C2 and then =C2+10 into D2 and copy that formula to the rest of the cells.)

11. Add fill color to Cells B3 through B7 and C2 through H2.

12. In Cell C3 type the following formula: =C$2*$B3.

13. Copy the formula from Cell C3 to cells C3 through H7.

14. Add All Borders around Cells C1 through H7 and around Cells A3 through B7.

15. Format Cells B3 through H7 as Currency.

The Intermediate
Excel Quiz Book

M.L. HUMPHREY

CONTENTS

INTRODUCTION

This is a companion book written to complement *Intermediate Excel* by M.L. Humphrey and is geared towards those who are already familiar with the content covered in that book who now want to test their knowledge through quizzes or to those who learn better from a question and answer format.

For each chapter in *Intermediate Excel* there is a set of questions meant to test your knowledge of the information that was covered in the chapter.

The first section of the book just has the questions, the next section of the book has the questions as well as the answers. There is also a bonus section that contains five exercises where you can test your knowledge of the various functions by applying them to specific real-life scenarios.

I encourage you to try to do each exercise first without looking at the solutions, since in the real world you'll be faced with a problem that needs solved and no one will be there to tell you how to solve it. However, I would also encourage you to have Excel open as you work each exercise so you can use the help functions within Excel to find what you need. Don't feel like you need to memorize every task in Excel in order to use it effectively. You just need to know what's possible and then what keywords or phrasing to use to help you find the information that will let you perform the right task.

Alright, then. Let's start with the first quiz.

QUIZZES

CONDITIONAL FORMATTING QUIZ

1. What does conditional formatting allow you to do?

2. Where can you find the Conditional Formatting option?

3. What conditional formatting options are available in Excel 2007?

4. If you want to mark all cells that have a value greater than $3,500, what conditional formatting option should you use?

5. If you want to mark all cells that have a value less than $1,500, what conditional formatting option should you use?

6. If you want to mark all cells that contain a certain text phrase, what conditional formatting option should you use?

7. If you want to flag when a value occurs more than once, what conditional formatting option can you use?

8. What is the issue with using the Duplicate Values conditional formatting option?

9. How can you customize the format that's applied to a range of cells when using conditional formatting for the greater than and less than rules?

10. If you want to flag the top 10 values in your range of data, which conditional formatting option can you use to do that?

11. Is it possible to flag just the top 5 values? If so, how?

12. What if you want to flag the top 10% of your results using conditional formatting, how can you do that?

13. Can you flag any % of your results?

14. How would you flag results that are above the average value for the range using conditional formatting?

15. How would you flag results that are below the average value for the range using conditional formatting?

16. What do Data Bars do?

17. What do Color Scales do?

18. What do Icon Sets do?

19. Can you customize the limits Excel uses when applying data bars, color scales, and icon sets? How?

20. How can you remove conditional formatting from a range of cells?

21. What if you only want to remove one conditional formatting rule from a range of cells, how can you do that?

22. How do you change the order in which conditional formatting rules are applied to a cell or range of cells?

23. What other option do you have for adding a new conditional formatting rule to your data other than using one of the pre-defined options (Highlight Cells Rules, Top/Bottom Rules, etc.)?

INSERTING SYMBOLS QUIZ

1. How do you insert a symbol into a cell in Excel?

2. Can you insert a symbol into a cell that already has text in it?

3. Which font has a lot of images like scissors, mailboxes, smiley faces, etc?

4. If you need the copyright symbol or trademark symbol, where can you find those?

5. Can you change the size or color of a symbol you've inserted? If so, how?

6. Once you've inserted a symbol into a cell can you change the font without impacting the symbol?

PIVOT TABLES QUIZ

1. What does a pivot table allow you to do?

2. How do you need to format your data in order to use a pivot table?

3. What are some best practices when formatting your data for analysis?

4. How do you start a pivot table?

5. Should you add your pivot table to your existing sheet or to a new one? Why?

6. What are the two ways you can add a field to your blank pivot table?

7. If you drag a field to the Filters section, what can you do with that field?

8. If you drag a field to the Rows section, how will that field appear in the table?

9. If you drag a field to the Columns section, how will that field appear in the table?

10. If you drag a field to the Values section, how will that field appear in the table?

11. How can you change the function that is performed on a field that you've placed in the Values section?

12. What functions can you apply to a field in the Values section?

13. If you want to format the values in your table, what are two ways to do so?

14. Can you perform two or more calculations on the same field in a pivot table? If so, how?

15. Can you have multiple fields for your rows or columns?

16. What would be the drawback in doing so?

17. Can you filter which results show for your rows or columns fields? For example, if you just wanted to see one customer's results in the rows section, could you do that? How?

18. Can you reorder the fields in the rows or columns section?

19. How can you get the PivotTable tools menu options to display?

20. What does the Group tool do under Analyze under PivotTable Tools?

21. How do you do this?

22. How do you remove a grouping?

23. If you do have a set of results grouped, how do you see the totals for that group?

24. If you have a set of results grouped and are only able to see the summary for the group, how do you make the individual results visible?

25. If you have multiple groups that you want to collapse to the summary level, how can you do this?

26. If you have multiple groups that you want to expand at once, how can you do this?

27. What does the Slicer do?

28. How do you reset any fields you've filtered using the Slicer?

29. What does Insert Timeline let you do?

30. What does Refresh do?

31. Why is Refresh useful?

32. What issue could you run into using Refresh that you need to be careful about?

33. What option can you use to change the data that's being used in your pivot table?

34. When might you want to change your data in your pivot table?

35. What should you watch out for when updating your data source?

36. What option can you use to clear your currently selected fields from your pivot table and return to a blank pivot table?

37. What option can you use to just clear any filters you've applied to your pivot table?

38. If you want to calculate the value of one field in your table times another field in your table, what's the best way to do this? Where is that option located?

39. What does the Design tab under PivotTable Tools allow you to do?

40. Name two ways you can remove a field you've added to a pivot table that you decide you don't want.

41. How can you change the order of the fields when you have multiple fields for Row, Column, or Value?

42. Can you write formulas that reference cells within a pivot table?

43. If you have generated a pivot table and want to use that data elsewhere but don't want to risk having the data update on you, what can you do?

44. Is it advisable to create a pivot table and then do calculations on the values of that pivot table outside of the table while leaving it in pivot table format? Why or why not?

SUBTOTALING AND GROUPING DATA QUIZ

1. What does the Subtotal option let you do?

2. Where is the Subtotal option located?

3. What must you do before you can subtotal your data?

4. What will happen if you try to subtotal unsorted data?

5. How do you subtotal data?

6. Which field in the Subtotal dialogue box is for the field you want to separate your data by?

7. Is this the only field Excel will perform the subtotal function on?

8. Can you perform different functions on different fields when you subtotal?

9. What functions can you choose to perform using subtotal?

10. How do you choose which fields to apply the function to?

11. Does the field you subtotal by also have to be a field you apply a function to?

12. Can it be?

13. What will checking the box for "page break between groups" do?

14. What will checking the box for "summary below data" do?

15. Once you've subtotaled your data, what do the numbers at the left-hand side of the row numbers do?

16. How do you remove subtotals?

17. What if you want to keep the subtotals you created, but just remove the grouping options on the left-hand side of the worksheet?

18. What does the Group option allow you to do? Where is it located?

19. When might you use this?

20. How do you group a set of rows or columns?

21. What is one requirement for any set of rows or columns you want to group?

22. If you've successfully grouped a set of rows or columns, how will you know?

23. How can you hide a set of grouped columns or rows?

24. How can you reveal a set of grouped columns or rows that are currently hidden?

25. How can you remove all grouping from a worksheet?

26. Should you use Ctrl + Z and Ctrl + Y when using subtotaling or grouping?

CHART TYPES QUIZ

1. What makes charts so useful?

2. How should you configure your data for most charts?

3. Once you have your data input in Excel, how can you create a chart of it?

4. How can you preview what your chart will look like?

5. What is time series data?

6. Which chart options are best for use with time series data?

7. For data with multiple variables (such as multiple vendors) but no time component (so 2018 summary, for example), what are the best chart options to use?

8. What are scatter plots good for?

9. What is the difference between a column chart and a bar chart in Excel?

10. What does a clustered columns graph do?

11. What are the advantages/disadvantages of a clustered column graph?

12. What does the stacked columns graph do?

13. What are the advantages/disadvantages of a stacked columns graph?

14. What does the 100% stacked column graph do?

15. What are the advantages/disadvantages of a 100% stacked column graph?

16. Is there generally a reason to use 3-D graphs in your presentations?

17. What is a pie chart?

18. What is the difference between a pie chart and a doughnut chart?

19. What does a pie of pie chart do?

20. What does a bar of pie chart do?

21. Which is generally better to use if you must use one, the pie of pie chart or the bar of pie chart?

22. What should you do with your data before using a scatter plot with lines in Excel? Why?

23. What is the difference between a scatter plot that uses smooth lines and one that uses straight lines?

24. What is the difference between a scatter plot with markers and one that doesn't have them?

25. Can you plot more than one set of results on a scatter plot at once? How?

EDITING CHARTS QUIZ

1. If the chart you just created has the wrong data points in the wrong places (so maybe it's showing vendor along the axis instead of month), what's one way you can attempt to fix that?

2. If you accidentally included a summary row in your chart, how can you easily fix that?

3. If you want to add another data point, for example, a new vendor to your existing graph, how can you do that?

4. If you want to expand the data points that are included in your chart, how can you do that?

5. How can you change the order in which the elements in your chart display?

6. How can you change your chart type?

7. What are Chart Styles?

8. How can you apply a Chart Style to a chart?

9. Do you have to select a Chart Style to see what it will look like with your data?

10. Does a Chart Style have to be exactly what you want for you to use it?

11. What is a Quick Layout?

12. How can you apply a Quick Layout to your chart?

13. Do you have to click on a Quick Layout option to see what it will look like on your chart?

14. Can you further customize a chart after you've applied a Quick Layout to it?

15. Can you use both a Chart Style and Quick Layout on the same chart? If so, what challenges are there to doing so?

16. What's the easiest way to change the colors in your chart?

17. What chart elements can you add or delete from a chart?

18. Where can you go under Chart Tools to add chart elements to your chart?

19. What does the Axes option allow you to do?

20. What does the Axis Titles option allow you to do?

21. When you use Axis Titles, is the title for that axis already populated?

22. What does Chart Title allow you to do?

23. What does Data Labels allow you to do?

24. When can Data Labels be particularly useful?

25. What does Data Table allow you to do?

26. What does Gridlines let you do?

27. What does Legend do?

28. What does Trendline allow you to do?

29. How can you change the size of your chart?

30. How can you move a chart to a new position within your worksheet?

31. How can you move a chart to a new worksheet or other document?

32. How can you manually rearrange the elements within a chart, such as the chart title?

33. Can you move all elements in a chart?

34. How do you change the title of a chart?

35. How do you change the name of a data field that's displayed in the legend of your chart?

36. How can you apply custom colors to your chart elements?

37. When should you use Shape Fill?

38. When should you use Shape Outline?

39. What do you need to be careful of when applying custom colors to your chart?

40. If you mess up, what's the easiest way to fix it?

41. What does the Formatting Task Pane do?

42. If you want to have the segments in your pie chart separated to make them more clearly visible, where can you go to do this?

43. Can you use the Home tab Font options to edit the font color, size, or style in a chart?

REMOVING DUPLICATE ENTRIES QUIZ

1. If you have a column that has duplicate values and you want to narrow the list down to just unique values, how can you do that?

2. In the Remove Duplicates dialogue box, what does checking the "my data has headers" box do?

3. When you have Excel remove duplicates from a single column of data what happens to that data?

4. Can you remove duplicate values across multiple columns?

5. How does that work?

6. Can you remove duplicates from two out of six columns in a data range? Should you?

7. Why should you always do any calculations or manipulations on a copy of your source data instead of the original copy?

CONVERTING TEXT TO COLUMNS QUIZ

1. What does Text to Columns allow you to do?

2. What is the most basic use of Text to Columns?

3. Before you apply Text to Columns to a column of data what should you do?

4. If I have a list of entries in Column A that are first name space last name, so "Mark Jones", "Dave Clark", etc. how can I separate that list into two columns, one with first name and one with last name and with no extra spaces?

5. If I have a list of entries in Column A where each entry starts with a two-digit number that indicates the year and is followed by a five-digit customer ID, how can I separate the two-digit year into one column and the five-digit ID into another column?

6. When you use the Delimiter option, what happens to your delimiter?

7. How can you delete a break line you placed that you don't want to use?

8. How can you move a break line you placed that isn't in the right location?

9. Can you choose more than one delimiter (say a space and a comma) under the Delimiter option?

10. Can you specify a custom delimiter? How?

11. Can you specify how you're newly-separated data will be formatted? How?

12. What do you need to be careful of when using the Delimiter option with Convert Text to Columns?

13. What function allows you to remove excess spaces from around text?

CONCATENATE QUIZ

1. What does the CONCATENATE function let you do?

2. What is the basic format of a CONCATENATE function?

3. Let's say you have customer first name in Cell A1, customer last name in Cell B1, and that you want to create an entry that's "LastName, FirstName" (last name comma space first name) using those values. How would you write that using the CONCATENATE function?

4. How would you create an entry that's "FirstName Last Name" (first name space last name)?

5. What would be the result be from the function =CONCATENATE("Jones",", ","Albert")? What does the ", " portion in the center represent? And why do we need the quotation marks around Jones and Albert?

6. After you've used the CONCATENATE function to create an entry, what do you need to be careful about with respect to the entry you've created?

7. How can you address this issue?

THE IF FUNCTION QUIZ

1. What does an IF function do?

2. Translate the IF function =IF(A2>25,0,A2*0.05) into a written description.

3. What is another way to think about the components of an IF function?

4. What does it mean that you can nest IF functions?

5. If you're going to nest IF functions, which is it better to replace, the Then portion or the Else portion? Why?

6. Translate the IF function =IF(A9>$A$5,$B$5,IF(A9>$A$4,$B$4,0)) into a written description.

7. If you were to copy the above formula into a new cell, how would it change?

8. If you have a long and complex nested IF function that you can't get to work, what are some ways you can troubleshoot the IF function to figure out what's wrong?

9. What is the most likely issue if Excel tells you you've entered too many arguments with an IF function?

10. What should you always do with an IF function that you create? (Or any function really?)

11. If you write an IF function that's referencing a table of fixed values (like a discount table) what should you always be sure to do?

COUNTIFS QUIZ

1. What does the COUNTIFS function do?

2. How does this differ from the COUNTIF function?

3. Which should you use?

4. What is the following function doing:
   =COUNTIFS(B2:B6,"Alaska")

5. What is the following function doing:
   =COUNTIFS(A1:A10,">25")

6. What is the following function doing:
   =COUNTIFS(C10:C200,"*a*")

7. What is the following function doing:
   =COUNTIFS(C10:C200,"*e")

8. Could any of the above four examples also be written using the COUNTIF function?

9. What is the following function doing:
=COUNTIFS(C10:C200,"Alaska",D2:D200,"Whatsits")

10. Could you use COUNTIF with the above example?

11. What do you need to watch out for in terms of your cell ranges when using multiple count criteria?

12. Can you have a COUNTIFS function that includes a text criteria and a numeric criteria both?

13. If you write a COUNTIFS function that references the values in three separate columns, say Columns A, B, and C, how will Excel look at the data to make its count. For example, with the formula

  =COUNTIFS(A:A,"Alaska",B:B,"Whatsits",C:C,"Paid")

what is Excel going to look at to make its count?

14. If you write a COUNTIFS function that references the values in three separate rows, say Rows 1, 2 and 3, how will Excel look at the data to make its count. For example, with the formula

  =COUNTIFS(1:1,"Alaska",2:2,"Whatsits",3:3,"Paid")

what is Excel going to look at to make its count?

15. What is one thing you can do when setting up a COUNTIFS function to make sure it's working before you expand it to your entire worksheet?

SUMIFS QUIZ

1. What does the SUMIFS function do?

2. How does it differ from the SUMIF function?

3. When was it introduced?

4. If you start by writing a SUMIF function and realize you want to write a SUMIFS function, can you do that?

5. If you have access to both SUMIF and SUMIFS, which should you use?

6. Write a description of what =SUMIFS(A1:A10,B1:B10, "NZD",C1:C10,"") is saying.

7. How would you write a SUMIFS function to sum the values in Column C when the values in Column D are greater than 30 and the value in Column E is Smith?

8. Can you apply SUMIFS to a range of cells (so two columns and two rows) and not just a column or row?

9. If you can, what do you need to make sure of?

TEXT FUNCTION QUIZ

1. What does the TEXT function do?

2. If the value in Cell A1 is 5 and you use =TEXT(A1, "$0.00") what result will you get?

3. If the value in Cell A1 is 5 and you use =TEXT(A1, "#.00") what result will you get?

4. If the value in Cell A1 is 5 and you use =TEXT(A1, "#.#0") what result will you get?

5. If the value in Cell A1 is 5 and you use =TEXT(A1, "#.##") what result will you get?

6. If the value in Cell A1 is 4.235 and you use =TEXT(A1, "$0.00") what result will you get?

7. If the value in Cell A1 is 4.235 and you use =TEXT(A1, "#.00") what result will you get?

8. If the value in Cell A1 is 4.235 and you use =TEXT(A1, "#.#0") what result will you get?

9. If the value in Cell A1 is 4.235 and you use =TEXT(A1, "#.##") what result will you get?

10. What is the difference between using a 0 and a # sign in the above examples?

11. What do you need to watch for when using the # sign for formatting?

12. If the value in Cell A1 is 4.235 and you use =TEXT(A1,"$#.##") & " per unit" what result will you get?

13. How can you take a date from Cell A1 and display its day of the week written fully? For example, Sunday.

14. How can you display its abbreviated day of the week? For example, Sun.

15. How can you isolate what day of the month it is from a date in Cell A1?

16. How can you take a date from Cell A1 and display its month of the year written fully? For example, November.

17. How can you display its abbreviated month of the year? For example, Nov.

18. How can you isolate the number for the month of the year from a date in Cell A1?

19. How can you isolate the year from a date in Cell A1?

LIMITING ALLOWED INPUTS QUIZ

1. What is the issue that you run into if you let users enter data in any way they choose?

2. How can you get around this issue?

3. What issue can you run into if you provide a dropdown menu of choices?

4. What's one way around this?

5. What's one danger of doing this?

6. How can you limit the values someone can input into a cell in Excel (general)?

7. If you want to limit users to a list of accepted text entries, what option should you choose? How do you specify the list?

8. If you want to limit users to only entering whole numbers, what option should you choose?

9. If you want users to be able to enter a decimal number instead, what option should you choose?

10. When limiting a user's input to a number (either whole or decimal), what else do you need to do? And what should you be careful about when doing so?

11. What will happen if you've applied data validation to a cell and a user tries to input an answer that isn't allowed?

12. Can you customize the message that displays? Where?

13. How can you remove data validation from a set of cells?

LOCKING CELLS OR WORKSHEETS QUIZ

1. Is it possible to keep users from editing the contents of cells in a worksheet? If so, how?

2. What do you need to watch out for when locking a worksheet?

3. How can you remove protection from a worksheet?

4. Is it possible to hide the contents of cells in a worksheet as well? How?

HIDING A WORKSHEET QUIZ

1. How can you hide a worksheet?

2. How can you unhide a worksheet?

3. How can you hide a worksheet and keep someone from unhiding it?

TWO-VARIABLE ANALYSIS
GRID QUIZ

1. What does a two-variable analysis grid let you do?

2. What shortcut can you use to make it easy to create a two-variable analysis grid?

3. How can you combine a two-variable analysis grid with conditional formatting?

MORE ANSWERS QUIZ

1. What are three ways that you can find out more information on a topic from within Excel?

2. What's the best way to find a function or learn more about a function you want to use?

3. If you need more information than that, what options do you have outside of Excel?

4. When is it better to use a forum than go to the Microsoft website?

5. What's a nice trick you can use when troubleshooting a function?

6. If you do something you didn't want to do, what's the easiest way to reverse it?

7. What's a best practice if you're building a really complex worksheet or one with lots of moving parts?

8. If you're using dates in your files names why use the YYYYMMDD format to record the date?

QUIZ ANSWERS

CONDITIONAL FORMATTING QUIZ ANSWERS

1. What does conditional formatting allow you to do?

It allows you to apply special formatting to cells that meet the criteria that you specify.

2. Where can you find the conditional formatting option?

In the Styles section of the Home tab.

3. What Conditional Formatting options are available in Excel 2007?

Highlight Cells Rules, Top/Bottom Rules, Data Bars, Color Scales, and Icon Sets.

4. If you want to mark all cells that have a value greater than $3,500, what conditional formatting option should you use?

Highlight Cells Rules, Greater Than

5. If you want to mark all cells that have a value less than $1,500, what conditional formatting option should you use?

Highlight Cells Rules, Less Than

6. If you want to mark all cells that contain a certain text phrase, what conditional formatting option should you use?

Highlight Cells Rules, Text that Contains

7. If you want to flag when a value occurs more than once, what conditional formatting option can you use?

Highlight Cells Rules, Duplicate Values

8. What is the issue with using the Duplicate Values conditional formatting option?

It highlights all cells in the range where a value occurs more than once and doesn't distinguish between different values. So a range of cells with more than one "ABC" and more than one "DEF" would have all cells that contain "ABC" and "DEF" flagged the same. This limits its immediate usefulness.

9. How can you customize the format that's applied to a range of cells when using conditional formatting for the greater than and less than rules?

In the Greater Than or Less Than dialogue boxes there are dropdowns that allow you to choose from six pre-defined formats. At the bottom of that list of formats you can also click on Custom Format which will open a Format Cells dialogue box that allows you to choose any formatting you want to apply to the cells.

10. If you want to flag the top 10 values in your range of data, which conditional formatting option can you use to do that?

Top/Bottom Rules, Top 10 Items

11. Is it possible to flag just the top 5 values? If so, how?

Yes. Use the Top/Bottom Rules, Top 10 Items, but change the number to 5 instead of 10.

12. What if you want to flag the top 10% of your results using conditional formatting, how can you do that?

Top/Bottom Rules, Top 10%

13. Can you flag any % of your results?

Yes. Just use the Top/Bottom Rules, Top 10% option, and change the percentage to the one you want to use.

14. How would you flag results that are above the average value for the range using conditional formatting?

Top/Bottom Rules, Above Average

15. How would you flag results that are below the average value for the range using conditional formatting?

Top/Bottom Rules, Below Average

16. What do Data Bars do?

Data bars overlay a bar onto a cell based upon its value. The higher the value in the cell relative to the rest of the values in the selected range, the larger the bar.

17. What do Color Scales do?

Color scales overlay a color onto a cell based upon the cell's relative value in relation to the rest of the cells in the selected range. Depending on the option chosen, higher values can be the darkest color in the range or the lightest color in the range. Also, some color scale options use multiple colors so the lowest value might be green while the highest value is red or vice versa.

18. What do Icon Sets do?

Icon sets allow you to display symbols in cells based on their values relative to the other values within the selected range. The symbols you can choose from include colored flags, arrows, or other shapes as well as bars, circles, and stars that are filled in as the value increases relative to the range.

19. Can you customize the limits Excel uses when applying data bars, color scales, and icon sets? How?

Yes. Set up your formatting and then go to Manage Rules under the Conditional Formatting dropdown in the Styles section of the Home tab and choose to Edit the rule. This will bring up a dialogue box where you can then change the criteria to what you want to use.

20. How can you remove conditional formatting from a range of cells?

To remove all formatting from a range of cells, highlight the cells, go to the Style section of the Home tab, click on Conditional Formatting, choose Clear Rules and then choose to clear the rules either from the selected cells or from the entire worksheet.

21. What if you only want to remove one conditional formatting rule from a range of cells, how can you do that?

Select the cells, go the Conditional Formatting dropdown menu, choose Manage Rules, and then delete the rule that you no longer want. You can also just go straight to Manage Rules and edit the range of cells covered by that particular rule.

22. How do you change the order in which conditional formatting rules are applied to a cell or range of cells?

Using the Manage Rules option under the Conditional Formatting dropdown and moving the rules listed for the worksheet into the order you prefer using the up and down arrows.

23. What other option do you have for adding a new conditional formatting rule to your data other than using one of the pre-defined options (Highlight Cells Rules, Top/Bottom Rules, etc.)?

You can also just go to New Rule under the Conditional Formatting dropdown menu. This will bring up the New Formatting Rule dialogue box which will let you specify the type of conditional formatting rule you want to use, the colors, and the values.

INSERTING SYMBOLS
QUIZ ANSWERS

1. How do you insert a symbol into a cell in Excel?

Click into the cell where you want to insert the symbol, go to the Symbols section of the Insert tab, and click on Symbol. This will bring up the Symbol dialogue box. Click on the symbol you want and then click Insert.

2. Can you insert a symbol into a cell that already has text in it?

Yes. Just use the formula bar to click into the location in the existing text for that cell where you want to insert the symbol.

3. Which font has a lot of images like scissors, mailboxes, smiley faces, etc?

Wingdings

4. If you need the copyright symbol or trademark symbol, where can you find those?

The Special Characters tab in the Symbol dialogue box.

5. Can you change the size or color of a symbol you've inserted? If so, how?

Yes. Just highlight it or the cell it's in and then use the options in the Font section of the Home tab.

6. Once you've inserted a symbol into a cell can you change the font without impacting the symbol?

Often times, no. The symbol you've inserted will be tied to the font used and if you change the font the symbol will be replaced by a normal character such as the * sign or [sign. For example, the yin yang sign in Wingdings is actually just the [character in Times New Roman.

PIVOT TABLES
QUIZ ANSWERS

1. What does a pivot table allow you to do?

Take a large amount of data and easily summarize it.

2. How do you need to format your data in order to use a pivot table?

There needs to be a header row that contains labels for each column of data. Below that your data should be arranged in rows with all data for a particular entry contained in that one row. There should be no summary rows or sub-totals in your data. Also remove any blank rows or columns from the data and make sure that you only have one type of data (date, currency, text) in each column.

3. What are some best practices when formatting your data for analysis?

Have a separate column for each data point you might want to analyze. So if you sell blue and green widgets and whatsits, have a column for product color as well as a column for product type. Also try to have standardized values as much as possible. Widgets should always be widgets. Make sure each row of data has all the information you need in it. This may mean repeating information like customer name in multiple rows, but that's okay.

4. How do you start a pivot table?

Highlight your data, go to the Insert tab, and choose Pivot Table from the Tables section.

5. Should you add your pivot table to your existing sheet or to a new one? Why?

Ideally you should add the pivot table to a new worksheet because pivot tables are dynamic and so can expand in terms of number of rows or columns. By adding the pivot table to a new worksheet you ensure that you won't overwrite any existing data.

6. What are the two ways you can add a field to your blank pivot table?

Left-click and drag the field to the spot in the pivot table where you want that field to be. Or left-click and drag the field to the Filters, Rows, Columns, or Values section, whichever you want to use, that's at the bottom of the PivotTable Fields box where it says "Drag fields between areas below."

7. If you drag a field to the Filters section, what can you do with that field?

The field will not appear in the pivot table, but there will be a dropdown menu that allows you to filter the table so that only specified results from that field are included in the table.

8. If you drag a field to the Rows section, how will that field appear in the table?

The values for that field will appear in the table on the left-hand side in rows.

9. If you drag a field to the Columns section, how will that field appear in the table?

The values for that field will appear across the top of the table in columns.

10. If you drag a field to the Values section, how will that field appear in the table?

Excel will calculate a value for that field based upon the intersection of the fields you've placed in the Rows and Columns sections and on any criteria you've filtered by. What value is calculated (sum, count, etc.) will be determined by what you choose.

11. How can you change the function that is performed on a field that you've placed in the Values section?

In the Pivot Table Fields box where you've placed the field, there should be a listing of the field that says something like "Count of [Field Name]" or "Sum of [Field Name]" which tells you what function is currently being performed on that field. Click on the arrow on the right-hand side of the name and choose Value Field Settings. This will bring up the Value Field Settings dialogue box where you can then change the function.

12. What functions can you apply to a field in the Values section?

Sum, Count, Average, Max, Min, Product, Count Numbers, Standard Deviation. You can also choose to show values as a % of the grand total, % of the column total, or % of the row total as well as some other options.

13. If you want to format the values in your table, what are two ways to do so?

You could just highlight the cells and use the formatting options in the Number section of the Home tab. Or you can use the Value Field Settings dialogue box, click on Number Format in the bottom left corner, and format the cells that way.

14. Can you perform two or more calculations on the same field in a pivot table? If so, how?

Yes. You just need to add the field to the Values section for each calculation you want to perform and then change the Value Field Settings to reflect the different calculations you want.

15. Can you have multiple fields for your rows or columns?

Yes.

16. What would be the drawback in doing so?

It can get messy pretty quickly if you have multiple fields in your rows, columns, and values sections.

17. Can you filter which results show for your rows or columns fields? For example, if you just wanted to see one customer's results in the rows section, could you do that? How?

Yes. Use the arrows next to Row Labels and Column Labels to bring up the list of values and uncheck the ones you don't want displayed.

18. Can you reorder the fields in the rows or columns section?

Yes.

19. How can you get the PivotTable tools menu options to display?

Click on your pivot table.

20. What does the Group tool do under Analyze under PivotTable Tools?

It allows you to create an artificial grouping of entries by clicking on each of the items that you want to include in your group.

21. How do you do this?

Hold down the Ctrl key while choosing all the items you want to group together and then choose Group Selection from the Group section of the Analyze tab. You can also choose the items and then right-click and choose Group from the dropdown menu.

22. How do you remove a grouping?

Click on the group name and then choose Ungroup from the Group section of the Analyze tab. You can also right-click and choose Ungroup from the dropdown.

23. If you do have a set of results grouped, how do you see the totals for that group?

Click on the minus sign next to the group name to collapse the entries down to the group level.

24. If you have a set of results grouped and are only able to see the summary for the group, how do you make the individual results visible?

Click on the + sign next to the group name.

25. If you have multiple groups that you want to collapse to the summary level, how can you do this?

Click on Collapse Field in the Active Field section of the Analyze tab.

26. If you have multiple groups that you want to expand at once, how can you do this?

Click on Expand Field in the Active Field section of the Analyze tab.

27. What does the Slicer do?

It works like a filter option, but it's visible to the user.

28. How do you reset any fields you've filtered using the Slicer?

Click on the funnel at the top of the window for the Slicer to clear any filter you have in place.

29. What does Insert Timeline let you do?

Filter the data in your pivot table by month, quarter, year, or day assuming you have a field that Excel recognizes as a date.

30. What does Refresh do?

It allows you to update your pivot table after you've updated your source data.

31. Why is Refresh useful?

Because you may find that your original data has small discrepancies in it, like using Albert Jones and Albert R. Jones, for the same customer and it's much easier to be able to fix those discrepancies and then refresh your table than to rebuild the table from scratch.

32. What issue could you run into using Refresh that you need to be careful about?

Pivot tables are dynamic, meaning they have a variable number of rows and columns in them based upon the data they're displaying. That means each time you refresh a pivot table the number of rows or columns may change and your data may shift. If you've made notes or calculations on the worksheet but outside of the pivot table they may no longer be accurate or they may be erased.

33. What option can you use to change the data that's being used in your pivot table?

Change Data Source.

34. When might you want to change your data in your pivot table?

When you add data for a new month, for example.

35. What should you watch out for when updating your data source?

Sometimes, especially if you try to use the arrow keys, Excel will insert new cell references into the existing cell references, thus ruining the cell range referenced as the data source. It's best, if possible, to just use your cursor to select the range of cells you want.

36. What option can you use to clear your currently selected fields from your pivot table and return to a blank pivot table?

Under the Analyze tab of PivotTable Tools select Clear and then Clear All.

37. What option can you use to just clear any filters you've applied to your pivot table?

Under the Analyze tab of PivotTable Tools select Clear and then Clear Filters.

38. If you want to calculate the value of one field in your table times another field in your table, what's the best way to do this? Where is that option located?

Insert Calculated Field. Located under Fields, Items & Sets.

39. What does the Design tab under PivotTable Tools allow you to do?

Choose how your pivot table displays. It allows you to change the colors, add divider rows, choose when and how to display subtotals, choose when and how to display grand totals, and change the formatting of your row or column headers.

40. Name two ways you can remove a field you've added to a pivot table that you decide you don't want.

Click on the arrow next to the field name in the bottom right corner of the PivotTable Fields table options and choose Remove Field. Or right-click in a cell in the pivot table that contains information from that field and choose "Remove [Field Name]" from the dropdown menu where [Field Name] represents the field you want to remove.

41. How can you change the order of the fields when you have multiple fields for Row, Column, or Value?

Left-click and drag the field to the order you want in the PivotTable Fields table. Or right-click on a cell that contains data for the field you want to move and then go to Move and choose the Move option you want.

42. Can you write formulas that reference cells within a pivot table?

Yes, but it's not easy to do and you can't copy the formulas the same way you would a normal formula because of the way cells in pivot tables are referenced.

43. If you have generated a pivot table and want to use that data elsewhere but don't want to risk having the data update on you, what can you do?

Select All, Copy, and Paste Special – Values. This will convert your pivot table into a simple table of data that can no longer be updated.

44. Is it advisable to create a pivot table and then do calculations on the values of that pivot table outside of the table while leaving it in pivot table format? Why or why not?

No. Because pivot tables are dynamic and can change their rows and columns when updated which can make any external calculations inaccurate or misaligned.

SUBTOTALING AND GROUPING DATA QUIZ ANSWERS

1. What does the Subtotal option let you do?

Take your data and summarize it at each change in a criteria that you specify.

2. Where is the Subtotal option located?

In the Outline section of the Data tab.

3. What must you do before you can subtotal your data?

You must sort your data so that all of the entries you want to subtotal by are grouped together. If you're subtotaling by year, then you want to sort by year. If you're subtotaling by customer, then you want to sort by customer.

4. What will happen if you try to subtotal unsorted data?

Excel will subtotal your data at every change in that criteria. Meaning you might end up with two subtotals for 2013 or three subtotals for Customer Albert Jones, because the entries weren't grouped together, so Excel treated each change as a new grouping.

5. How do you subtotal data?

Select all of the data you want to use, click on Subtotal in the Outline section of the Data tab to bring up the Subtotal dialogue box, and then tell Excel which field to subtotal by, what function to apply when it does so, and which fields to apply that function to.

6. Which field in the Subtotal dialogue box is for the field you want to separate your data by?

The "at each change in" field.

7. Is this the only field Excel will perform the subtotal function on?

No. This is the field that triggers Excel to "subtotal" the data, but it doesn't have to be the field that's subtotaled nor does it have to be the only field that's subtotaled.

8. Can you perform different functions on different fields when you subtotal?

No. You can only perform one function on all of the fields you choose.

9. What functions can you choose to perform using subtotal?

Sum, Count, Average, Max, Min, Product, Count Numbers, StdDev, StdDevp, Var, Varp. (Note that in the guide only the functions up to Product were listed. The rest of these options were pulled by looking in Excel.)

10. How do you choose which fields to apply the function to?

In the Subtotal dialogue box under "add subtotal to" the name of each of the selected fields will be listed. Click in the check box for each field where the function should be applied.

11. Does the field you subtotal by also have to be a field you apply a function to?

No.

12. Can it be?

Yes.

13. What will checking the box for "page break between groups" do?

It will insert a page break at every change in the criteria you chose to subtotal by. So if you chose customer name, then each time there was a change in customer name Excel would "subtotal" the data and insert a page break.

14. What will checking the box for "summary below data" do?

It will insert a Grand Total summary row at the very bottom of your data that shows the calculation of the function you selected for each field you selected for the entire data set.

15. Once you've subtotaled your data, what do the numbers at the left-hand side of the row numbers do?

They allow you to collapse your subtotaled data to the summary level. The 1 will display just the grand total, the 2 will display the subtotals and grand total, and the 3 will display all entries as well as the subtotals and grand total.

16. How do you remove subtotals?

Click on the Subtotal option in the Outline section of the Data tab to bring up the Subtotal dialogue box and choose Remove All.

17. What if you want to keep the subtotals you created, but just remove the grouping options on the left-hand side of the worksheet?

You can either click on Ungroup in the Outline section

of the Data tab and then select Ungroup from the dropdown to remove one group at a time, or you can selected Clear Outline from the dropdown to remove all levels of grouping.

18. What does the Group option allow you to do? Where is it located?

It allows you to group a set of rows or columns so that they can easily be hidden from view and then brought back to view by a simple click on a plus/minus sign. It's located in the Outline section of the Data tab.

19. When might you use this?

When you have data in a table that you don't want to have regularly visible but that you expect you will want to see on occasion. As opposed to Hide Rows or Hide Columns, which are easy to remove but harder to put back in place, using grouping allows you to move back and forth between hidden and visible with ease.

20. How do you group a set of rows or columns?

Select the rows or columns you want to group, choose Group from the Outline section of the Data tab, and then choose Group from the dropdown menu.

21. What is one requirement for any set of rows or columns you want to group?

They must be adjacent to one another. You can't group non-contiguous rows or columns.

22. If you've successfully grouped a set of rows or columns, how will you know?

You'll see a line above the columns or to the left of the rows that has a minus sign at the end. You should also see numbers on the left-hand side of the worksheet showing the grouping levels now available in the worksheet.

23. How can you hide a set of grouped columns or rows?

Click on the minus sign at the end of the line above the columns or to the left of the rows.

24. How can you reveal a set of grouped columns or rows that are currently hidden?

Click on the plus sign above where the columns should be or to the left of where the rows should be.

25. How can you remove all grouping from a worksheet?

Use the Clear Outline option under Ungroup in the Outline section of the Data tab.

26. Should you use Ctrl + Z and Ctrl + Y when using subtotaling or grouping?

Probably not. It's possible that if you have two workbooks open Excel will undo something in your other workbook rather than undo something related to the subtotaling or grouping that you just did. If you do use them, be careful to confirm that whatever you wanted undone was actually undone and not something else.

CHART TYPES
QUIZ ANSWERS

1. What makes charts so useful?

They allow you to visualize your data which will sometimes reveal patterns or insights that aren't readily apparent when just looking at the numbers.

2. How should you configure your data for most charts?

Have a row of labels across the top, another of labels down the side, and record the value for the intersection of those two variables (for example, total sales for that vendor on that date) at the intersection of the two labels in the Excel table.

3. Once you have your data input in Excel, how can you create a chart of it?

Select the data you want to use, go to the Insert tab, and click on the chart type you want to use.

4. How can you preview what your chart will look like?

Instead of clicking on the chart type simply hold your mouse over the chart type you want to use and Excel will display the chart for you. The chart will not be added to your worksheet until you click on it, however.

5. What is time series data?

It's data that shows results over a period of time. So, for example, sales by vendor by month for the year.

6. Which chart options are best for use with time series data?

Column charts, bar charts, and line charts.

7. For data with multiple variables (such as multiple vendors) but no time component (so 2018 summary, for example), what are the best chart options to use?

Pie charts or doughnut charts.

8. What are scatter plots good for?

Random data points where you're looking at the intersection of two or three variables to see if there's a pattern or relationship between the variables.

9. What is the difference between a column chart and a bar chart in Excel?

A column chart has the data displayed in vertical columns. A bar chart has the data displayed in horizontal columns.

10. What does a clustered columns graph do?

The clustered columns graph shows a column for each variable (such as vendor) for each time period (such as month) side-by-side.

11. What are the advantages/disadvantages of a clustered column graph?

You can easily see the difference in results across each variable within a time period, however, if you have a number of variables that you're charting it can quickly become too busy to use.

12. What does the stacked columns graph do?

It displays a single column for each time period that is separated into colored bands where the height of each colored band represents the value for that variable for that time period. It basically takes the columns from the clustered columns graph for each time period and stacks them on top of one another.

13. What are the advantages/disadvantages of a stacked columns graph?

If you have a lot of variables, it's not as busy as the clustered columns graph. It lets you easily see the overall trend across time periods since the height of the column shows overall results for the period. It can sometimes be harder to see changes in individual results for different variables across time.

14. What does the 100% stacked column graph do?

It displays all results for a time period in a single column but instead of the column height being based on values for each variable, it's based on percent share of the whole for the time period. This means that across time periods the height of the column is the same, since the height of the column is always going to be 100%. The colored sections of the column for the time period are the percent that that variable represented of total units for the period.

15. What are the advantages/disadvantages of a 100% stacked column graph?

You can't see any change in value over time. So if you go from earning $10,000 in one period to earning $1,000 in the next but the relative share of earnings for each variable stays the same, you won't see any change in the graph. What it does show nicely is share of return for each variable. So if one variable goes from being 5% of your sales to 50% that will show clearly on a 100% stacked column graph.

16. Is there generally a reason to use 3-D graphs in your presentations?

No.

17. What is a pie chart?

A pie chart is a round chart that shows your results as slices of a pie where the size of each slice is based upon the percent share of the whole for that variable. For example, you might have a pie chart of annual sales at each vendor that shows how much of your revenue came from each one.

18. What is the difference between a pie chart and a doughnut chart?

A doughnut chart is just like a pie chart except it's just the outer edge of the chart and has no center to it.

19. What does a pie of pie chart do?

It takes a pie chart and for the smallest results it creates a second pie chart to display those results in more detail.

20. What does a bar of pie chart do?

It takes a pie chart and for the smallest results it creates a bar chart to display those results in more detail.

21. Which is generally better to use if you must use one, the pie of pie chart or the bar of pie chart?

A bar of pie chart, because there's less likely to be confusion in viewing the results. With a pie of pie chart it's easy to think that the size of the slices in the two pie charts are comparable, but they are not. The second pie chart is showing % of the small slice it was derived from, not % of the whole.

22. What should you do with your data before using a scatter plot with lines in Excel? Why?

Sort it. Because if you're using a scatter plot that includes lines between points, Excel will draw that line from the first point to the second point, etc. rather than try to draw a smooth line through the data points. If you don't sort your data and try to have Excel draw a line through the points you may get a criss-crossing mess on your graph instead of a smooth path between points.

23. What is the difference between a scatter plot that uses smooth lines and one that uses straight lines?

A smooth line plot will try to create a line that follows a curve between points. A straight line plot will draw a straight line between each point in the graph. Often the difference won't be all that noticeable.

24. What is the difference between a scatter plot with markers and one that doesn't have them?

A scatter plot with markers will place a dot on the graph for every data point. A scatter plot without them will just show the lines that connect the points. This can be an important distinction if you have a data point that's missing.

25. Can you plot more than one set of results on a scatter plot at once? How?

Yes. Just list the results side-by-side with the criteria you want as the horizontal axis listed first. (So Month, Candidate A, Candidate B with the results for each candidate at the intersection of the month's row and the candidate's column.)

EDITING CHARTS QUIZ ANSWERS

1. If the chart you just created has the wrong data points in the wrong places (so maybe it's showing vendor along the axis instead of month), what's one way you can attempt to fix that?

Use the Switch/Row Column option in the Data section of the Design tab under Chart Tools.

2. If you accidentally included a summary row in your chart, how can you easily fix that?

Go to Select Data in the Design tab under Chart Tools to bring up the Select Data Source dialogue box and uncheck the box for that summary row or highlight it and click Remove. You can also double-click on your chart and then go to the data table and click and drag the selected cells boundaries until that row is no longer selected.

3. If you want to add another data point, for example, a new vendor to your existing graph, how can you do that?

Go to Select Data in the Design tab under Chart Tools to bring up the Select Data Source dialogue box and then choose Add, name the series, and select the data you want to include. You can also double-click on the chart and then go to the data table and click and drag the selected cell boundaries until that new data is included.

4. If you want to expand the data points that are included in your chart, how can you do that?

Go to Select Data in the Design tab under Chart Tools to bring up the Select Data Source dialogue box, click on the series you want to edit, choose Edit, and then change the cell references to include the data points you want to include. You can also double-click on the chart and then go to the data table and click and drag the selected cell boundaries to include the new data points.

5. How can you change the order in which the elements in your chart display?

Go to Select Data in the Design tab under Chart Tools to bring up the Select Data Source dialogue box, click on the elements you want to move and use the up and down arrows to move them around.

6. How can you change your chart type?

Click on the chart and then go to the Insert tab and choose your new chart type. Or go to the Design tab under Chart Tools, choose Change Chart Type, and choose your chart type from there.

7. What are Chart Styles?

Pre-formatted templates for each chart type that include a variety of color options and various chart elements. They can be a quick way to format a chart if the elements and colors work for what you need.

8. How can you apply a Chart Style to a chart?

Click on the chart, go to the Design tab under Chart Tools, and look at the available options in the Chart Styles section of the tab. Click on the one you want.

9. Do you have to select a Chart Style to see what it will look like with your data?

No. You can just hold your mouse over the style and Excel will show you what the chart will look like using that style. It will not, however, permanently apply the style until you click on it.

10. Does a Chart Style have to be exactly what you want for you to use it?

No. You can start by applying a chart style and then customize it from there.

11. What is a Quick Layout?

The Quick Layout option is another option you have for formatting a chart that provides a variety of layout options to choose from that mostly involve different configurations of the axis labels, chart title, legend, etc. It will not change any of your chart colors like Chart Styles will.

12. How can you apply a Quick Layout to your chart?

Click on the chart and then go to the Design tab under Chart Tools and in the Chart Layouts section click on the Quick Layout dropdown and choose the layout you want.

13. Do you have to click on a Quick Layout option to see what it will look like on your chart?

No. You can hold your cursor over each option to see what it will look like before you actually apply it to your chart.

14. Can you further customize a chart after you've applied a Quick Layout to it?

Yes.

15. Can you use both a Chart Style and Quick Layout on the same chart? If so, what challenges are there to doing so?

Yes, but only if you do it in the right order. If you

choose Chart Style first and then use a Quick Layout you'll keep the color scheme and background colors from the Chart Style but the positioning of the chart elements from the Quick Layout. If you use the Quick Layout first, the Chart Style will overwrite the Quick Layout when you apply it.

16. What's the easiest way to change the colors in your chart?

Use Change Colors which provides you with pre-defined color palettes to choose from and is available in the Design tab under Chart Tools. (You can also use Shape Styles under the Format tab under Chart Tools to change the color of specific elements in your chart one at a time using pre-defined options.)

17. What chart elements can you add or delete from a chart?

Axes, Axis Titles, Chart Title, Data Labels, Data Table, Error Bars, Gridlines, Legend, Lines, Trendline, and Up/Down Bars

18. Where can you go under Chart Tools to add chart elements to your chart?

Under Add Chart Elements in the Chart Layouts section of the Design tab.

19. What does the Axes option allow you to do?

Add or delete data point labels to each axis of your chart. (So along the bottom or side of the chart.)

20. What does the Axis Titles option allow you to do?

Add a title to each axis of your chart. If there already is a title for an axis, you can also remove it.

21. When you use Axis Titles, is the title for that axis already populated?

No. It says "Axis Title". You'll need to click into the title box and replace that with the label you want.

22. What does Chart Title allow you to do?

Allows you to either remove the existing chart title or change where the title is located on the chart (at the top or overlaid on the chart itself).

23. What does Data Labels allow you to do?

Label each of the data points in your chart with its value.

24. When can Data Labels be particularly useful?

With pie charts where there aren't axes to show the values.

25. What does Data Table allow you to do?

Add or remove a table underneath your chart that shows the data that was used to create the chart. It can either include legend keys that let you tie the entries in the table to the chart using color-matching or not.

26. What does Gridlines let you do?

Add (or remove) horizontal or vertical lines to your chart which can make it easier to identify the approximate values represented in your chart.

27. What does Legend do?

Let you determine the location of the chart's legend, which is the color-coded guide that tells you what color represents what data point. It can be at the top, bottom, left, or right-hand side. You can also remove it entirely, but that's not recommended unless you're using a Data Table with Legend Keys.

28. What does Trendline allow you to do?

Add a line onto your line chart that shows the overall

trend in the data for that variable. (So, for a specific vendor, for example.)

29. How can you change the size of your chart?

Click on the chart and then left-click and drag on one of the white boxes along the perimeter of the chart. You can also click on the chart to pull up the Format Chart Area formatting task pane and then go to the Size & Properties option and input a size there.

30. How can you move a chart to a new position within your worksheet?

Left-click on an empty space within the chart, hold that left-click, and drag the chart to where you want it. (If you click on a chart element, you may end up moving the chart element instead of the chart.)

31. How can you move a chart to a new worksheet or other document?

Click on an empty space within the chart and then use Ctrl + C to copy the chart or Ctrl + V to cut it from its current location, go to where you want to place the chart, and use Ctrl + V to paste it there. (You can also use the other cut/copy/paste options like right-clicking and selecting from the dropdown or going to the Clipboard section of the Home tab. The control shortcuts are just the quickest way to do it.)

32. How can you manually rearrange the elements within a chart, such as the chart title?

Left-click on the element you want to move, hold that down, and drag it to where you want it.

33. Can you move all elements in a chart?

No. Not all of the elements will move.

34. How do you change the title of a chart?

Left-click on the chart title, click into the box to highlight the existing text, delete it, and add your own text.

35. How do you change the name of a data field that's displayed in the legend of your chart?

Your best approach is to do so in the original data table. When you do that the legend will update. (You could also go to the Select Data option in the Design tab under Chart Tools to bring up the Select Data Source dialogue box and then choose to Edit that element and change the Series name from a cell reference to text. If you do that, however, that creates a disconnect between your data table and your chart that you need to remember exists.)

36. How can you apply custom colors to your chart elements?

Use the Format Tab under Chart Tools to apply colors to each chart element separately. To do so, click on the element you want to change, go to the Format tab under Chart Tools, and click on Shape Fill or Shape Outline and then choose your color.

37. When should you use Shape Fill?

To change the color of the elements in bar, column, or pie charts. Or the interior of 3-D chart elements.

38. When should you use Shape Outline?

To change the color of the elements in a line graph or for the border of 3-D chart elements.

39. What do you need to be careful of when applying custom colors to your chart?

That you've only selected the portion of the chart that applies to one data element at a time. It's very easy to accidentally change the color of all chart elements at once, especially with pie charts.

40. If you mess up, what's the easiest way to fix it?

Ctrl + Z to undo and then try again.

41. What does the Formatting Task Pane do?

Gives you another way to edit your chart that sometimes has more options than the menu options available under Chart Tools.

42. If you want to have the segments in your pie chart separated to make them more clearly visible, where can you go to do this?

The Pie Explosion option under Series Options in the Format Data Series formatting task pane.

43. Can you use the Home tab Font options to edit the font color, size, or style in a chart?

Yes.

REMOVING DUPLICATE ENTRIES
QUIZ ANSWERS

1. If you have a column that has duplicate values and you want to narrow the list down to just unique values, how can you do that?

Use Remove Duplicates which is located in the Data Tools section of the Data tab.

2. In the Remove Duplicates dialogue box, what does checking the "my data has headers" box do?

It excludes the first row of your data from the analysis. If you don't check that box the first row will be treated just like any other row in your data.

3. When you have Excel remove duplicates from a single column of data what happens to that data?

You're left with one unique occurrence of each value and the data is consolidated into continuous rows. So if you had 100 entries in that column and there were ten unique values spread across the hundred rows, those ten values will now show as the first ten entries in the column no matter where they were located in the column before that.

4. Can you remove duplicate values across multiple columns?

Yes.

5. How does that work?

If you choose to remove duplicate values across Columns A and B then Excel will evaluate the combination of the values in Column A and B for each row to determine if duplicates exist. In that case, for example, you might end up with ABC Corp, Nevada and ABC Corp, New York as separate entries because they're unique combinations of the values in Columns A and B.

6. Can you remove duplicates from two out of six columns in a data range? Should you?

You can but you shouldn't. If you just select the two columns and remove duplicates Excel will consolidate those entries in those two columns so that they're no longer aligned with the data in the other four columns. If you select all six and choose to remove duplicates from two of the six, when Excel removes duplicates it will delete the data for the other four columns where duplicates existed. You'll end up losing data and having no real way to see that that happened.

7. Why should you always do any calculations or manipulations on a copy of your source data instead of the original copy?

Because there are some errors you cannot fix and will not know you have made until it's too late to undo them. By keeping a clean copy of your original data this allows you to always go back and start over from scratch. If you don't keep a clean copy of your original data you may do something to your data (like remove duplicates improperly) that you can't fix.

CONVERTING TEXT TO COLUMNS
QUIZ ANSWERS

1. What does Text to Columns allow you to do?

It allows you to take information that's all in one cell and split it out across multiple columns based upon the criteria you specify.

2. What is the most basic use of Text to Columns?

When dealing with a .csv file that has one long entry per row where each column's data is indicated by a comma. (Although more recent versions of Excel do this conversion for you automatically.)

3. Before you apply Text to Columns to a column of data what should you do?

Check to make sure that there is no information in the columns to the right of that column that will be overwritten when you apply Text to Columns.

4. If I have a list of entries in Column A that are first name space last name, so "Mark Jones", "Dave Clark", etc. how can I separate that list into two

columns, one with first name and one with last name and with no extra spaces?

Click on Column A, go to the Data Tools section of the Data tab and select Text to Columns. In the Convert Text to Columns Wizard dialogue box choose the Delimited option and then click Next. On the second screen choose Space and check the box so that consecutive delimiters are treated as one. Click Finish.

5. If I have a list of entries in Column A where each entry starts with a two-digit number that indicates the year and is followed by a five-digit customer ID, how can I separate the two-digit year into one column and the five-digit ID into another column?

Click on Column A, go to the Data Tools section of the Data tab and select Text to Columns. In the Convert Text to Columns Wizard dialogue box choose the Fixed Width option and then click Next. On the second screen click onto the data preview to put a break line after the first two digits in the number. Click Finish.

6. When you use the Delimiter option, what happens to your delimiter?

It's deleted.

7. How can you delete a break line you placed that you don't want to use?

Double-click on it.

8. How can you move a break line you placed that isn't in the right location?

Click on it and drag it to where you want it to go.

9. Can you choose more than one delimiter (say a space and a comma) under the Delimiter option?

Yes.

10. Can you specify a custom delimiter? How?

Yes. Check the Other box and then type in the delimiter you want to use.

11. Can you specify how you're newly-separated data will be formatted? How?

Yes. On the final screen of the Convert Text to Columns Wizard.

12. What do you need to be careful of when using the Delimiter option with Convert Text to Columns?

Not all data entries are the same dimensions and so using a delimiter may end up with one entry being split into three columns while another is split into two columns. This is especially true when working with a data set that wasn't built to be split. For example, if you have an employee "Mark Jones" and another who is "David Allen Marks" and you split those names using a space delimiter you will have Mark and Jones in two columns but then you will have David, Allen, and Marks in three columns and the middle name of David Allen Marks will be lined up with the last name of Mark Jones.

13. What function allows you to remove excess spaces from around text?

TRIM

CONCATENATE QUIZ ANSWERS

1. What does the CONCATENATE function let you do?

According to Excel it allows you to join several text strings into one. The strings of information you can combine include numbers, symbols, punctuation, and values in other cells.

2. What is the basic format of a CONCATENATE function?

=CONCATENATE(text1, [text2],…) where each element in the function is separated by a comma and each "text" entry can either be a cell reference or a text entry indicated by quotation marks at the beginning and the end of the text.

3. Let's say you have customer first name in Cell A1, customer last name in Cell B1, and that you want to create an entry that's "LastName, FirstName" (last name comma space first name) using those values. How would you write that using the CONCATENATE function?

=CONCATENATE(B1,", ",A1)

4. How would you create an entry that's "FirstName Last Name" (first name space last name)?
=CONCATENATE(A1," ",B1)

5. What would the result be from the function =CONCATENATE("Jones",", ","Albert")? What does the ", " portion in the center represent? And why do we need the quotation marks around Jones and Albert?
You would get:

Jones, Albert

The ", " portion adds a comma followed by a space in the middle of the two text entries. It's in quotation marks because it's referring to text. That's why there are quotation marks around Jones and Albert as well since they're text entries not cell references. A cell reference does not require quotation marks but text does.

6. After you've used the CONCATENATE function to create an entry, what do you need to be careful about with respect to the entry you've created?
It's still a function, which means that even though it looks like a text entry it's using other cells to create the entry. If you delete the other cells that are feeding into the function it will impact your CONCATENATE function as well and change what's displayed.

7. How can you address this issue?
Once your CONCATENATE entry looks the way you want it to, copy it and then Paste Special – Values so that the formula is removed and just the text remains.

THE IF FUNCTION QUIZ ANSWERS

1. What does an IF function do?

It allows you to return different results depending on whether the criteria you specify are met or not.

2. Translate the IF function =IF(A2>25,0,A2*0.05) into a written description.

IF Cell A2 has a value greater than 25 then return a value of zero. Otherwise, return a value equal to the value in Cell A2 times .05.

3. What is another way to think about the components of an IF function?

IF(If, Then, Else) or IF A, THEN B, ELSE C or IF A, THEN B, OTHERWISE C.

4. What does it mean that you can nest IF functions?

It means that you can start with one IF function and then replace either the THEN component or the ELSE component with another IF function so that you get IF A, THEN B, ELSE, IF C, THEN D, OTHERWISE E, for example.

5. If you're going to nest IF functions, which is it better to replace, the Then portion or the Else portion? Why?

The Else portion. Because then that keeps all of the parts of each individual IF function together as opposed to splitting them up across the function.

6. Translate the IF function =IF(A9>$A$5,$B$5, IF(A9>$A$4,$B$4,0)) into a written description.

If the value in Cell A9 is greater than the value in Cell A5, then return the value in Cell B5. Otherwise, if the value in Cell A9 is greater than the value in Cell A4, return the value in Cell B4. Otherwise return a value of zero.

7. If you were to copy the above formula into a new cell, how would it change?

The only thing that would change is the cell reference to cell A9, the rest of the function uses $ signs to refer to specified cells. It's using a table to generate the results of the IF function.

8. If you have a long and complex nested IF function that you can't get to work, what are some ways you can troubleshoot the IF function to figure out what's wrong?

Arrow through the function to make sure that you have the correct number of opening and closing parens. For each IF in the function there should be one opening paren immediately after the IF and a corresponding closing paren somewhere in the funtion.

Replace all but one of the IF functions with a placeholder result to create a simple IF function and evaluate whether it's doing what it should. So, for example, =IF(A9>$A$5,$B$5,IF(A9>$A$4,$B$4,0)) would become =IF(A9>$A$5,$B$5,"ELSE") where the second IF function has temporarily been replaced with a result of ELSE.

9. What is the most likely issue if Excel tells you you've entered too many arguments with an IF function?

You probably have a misplaced paren somewhere. (Older versions of Excel did limit the number of IF functions you could nest, but in current versions you're unlikely to have too many IF functions nested.)

10. What should you always do with an IF function that you create? (Or any function really?)

Test it to make sure it's doing what it should be. Pay particular attention to threshold results where the result should transition from one result to another. For example, did you mean greater than or did you mean greater than or equal to and how did you actually write it?

11. If you write an IF function that's referencing a table of fixed values (like a discount table) what should you always be sure to do?

Use $ signs when writing the references to those cells so that you can easily copy your IF function while keeping the table references fixed.

COUNTIFS QUIZ ANSWERS

1. What does the COUNTIFS function do?

It allows you to count how many times a set of criteria are met with a data set. So, for example, how many customers are from Alaska and buy Whatsits.

2. How does this differ from the COUNTIF function?

The COUNTIF function does the same thing but for only one criteria.

3. Which should you use?

If you have Excel 2007 or later, you should use COUNTIFS instead of COUNTIF because you can replicate the results of COUNTIF using COUNTIFS. Prior to Excel 2007 COUNTIFS did not exist so you'll be stuck with COUNTIF and unable to do the more complex counts available through using COUNTIFS.

4. What is the following function doing:
=COUNTIFS(B2:B6,"Alaska")

It is saying to count the number of entries in Cells B2 through B6 that have the text value Alaska.

5. What is the following function doing: =COUNTIFS(A1:A10,">25")

It is saying to count the number of entries in Cells A1 through A10 where the value is greater than 25.

6. What is the following function doing: =COUNTIFS(C10:C200,"*a*")

It is saying to count the number of entries in Cells C10 through C200 where the entry includes the letter a anywhere in the cell.

7. What is the following function doing: =COUNTIFS(C10:C200,"*e")

It is saying to count the number of entries in Cells C10 through C200 where the entry includes the letter e at the end of a word.

8. Could any of the above four examples also be written using the COUNTIF function?

Yes. Since they only have one count criteria, they could work equally well with COUNTIF.

9. What is the following function doing: =COUNTIFS (C10:C200,"Alaska",D10:D200,"Whatsits")

It is saying to count the number of entries in Rows 10 through 200 where the value in Column C is Alaska and the value in Column D is Whatsits.

10. Could you use COUNTIF with the above example?

No, because there are two count criteria.

11. What do you need to watch out for in terms of your cell ranges when using multiple count criteria?

That the cell ranges for each of your count criteria are the same dimensions. So the same number of rows down and/or columns across so that Excel can match the entries across your count criteria.

12. Can you have a COUNTIFS function that includes a text criteria and a numeric criteria both?

Yes.

13. If you write a COUNTIFS function that references the values in three separate columns, say Columns A, B, and C, how will Excel look at the data to make its count. For example, with the formula =COUNTIFS (A:A,"Alaska",B:B,"Whatsits",C:C,"Paid") what is Excel going to look at to make its count?

It's going to look at each Row to see if the values in each of those columns are Alaska, Whatsits, and Paid. Only if the columns in a row contain those results will Excel count the entry.

14. If you write a COUNTIFS function that references the values in three separate rows, say Rows 1, 2 and 3, how will Excel look at the data to make its count. For example, with the formula =COUNTIFS (1:1,"Alaska",2:2,"Whatsits",3:3,"Paid") what is Excel going to look at to make its count?

It's going to look at each Column to see if the values in each of those rows are Alaska, Whatsits, and Paid. Only if the rows in a column contain those results will Excel count the entry.

15. What is one thing you can do when setting up a COUNTIFS function to make sure it's working before you expand it to your entire worksheet?

Start with a smaller sample that only has a few variables that you can test for issues in your formula. But also be sure that you've tested all possible scenarios. So if your criteria is "*e" then make sure you've tested words that start with e, have an e in the middle, and end with e to see if the count you get is what you expected.

SUMIFS QUIZ ANSWERS

1. What does the SUMIFS function do?

It allows you to sum a value that you specify based upon whether one or more other criteria are met.

2. How does it differ from the SUMIF function?

SUMIFS allows you specify multiple criteria that must be met before a value is summed. SUMIF only allows you to specify one variable.

3. When was it introduced?

Excel 2007, so those who have older versions of Excel don't have access to SUMIFS, they only have access to SUMIF.

4. If you start by writing a SUMIF function and realize you want to write a SUMIFS function, can you do that?

No. The order of the arguments are different in a SUMIFS function than they are in a SUMIF function so you would have to start over.

5. If you have access to both SUMIF and SUMIFS, which should you use?

SUMIFS. Because SUMIF and SUMIFS order their variables differently it's a best practice to always use SUMIFS even if you have just one sum criteria.

6. Write a description of what =SUMIFS(A1:A10, B1:B10, "NZD",C1:C10,"") is saying?

To sum the values in each row in Column A when the value in Column B for that row is NZD and the cell in Column C for that row is blank.

7. How would you write a SUMIFS function to sum the values in Column C when the values in Column D are greater than 30 and the value in Column E is Smith?

=SUMIFS(C:C,D:D,">30",E:E,"Smith")

8. Can you apply SUMIFS to a range of cells (so two columns and two rows) and not just a column or row?

Yes.

9. If you can, what do you need to make sure of?

That the dimensions of all of your ranges are the same. So if your sum group is 2x2 then your criteria groups must also be 2x2.

TEXT FUNCTION QUIZ ANSWERS

1. What does the TEXT function do?

According to Excel the TEXT function "converts a value to text in a specific format" but it's also a way to convert date entries to their day of the week or month of the year equivalents and to format a number.

2. If the value in Cell A1 is 5 and you use =TEXT(A1, "$0.00") what result will you get?

$5.00

3. If the value in Cell A1 is 5 and you use =TEXT(A1, "#.00") what result will you get?

5.00

4. If the value in Cell A1 is 5 and you use =TEXT(A1, "#.#0") what result will you get?

5.0

5. If the value in Cell A1 is 5 and you use =TEXT(A1, "#.##") what result will you get?

5.

6. If the value in Cell A1 is 4.235 and you use =TEXT (A1,"$0.00") what result will you get?

   $4.24

7. If the value in Cell A1 is 4.235 and you use =TEXT (A1,"#.00") what result will you get?

   4.24

8. If the value in Cell A1 is 4.235 and you use =TEXT (A1,"#.#0") what result will you get?

   4.24

9. If the value in Cell A1 is 4.235 and you use =TEXT (A1,"#.##") what result will you get?

   4.24

10. What is the difference between using a 0 and a # sign in the above examples?

A zero will force a specified number of decimal places to show even if they're not needed. This is why the examples with .00 and the value of 5 return 5.00 as a result. A pound sign will display up to that number of decimal places but won't force them if they're not needed. That's why the example with the #.## and the 5 doesn't have any numbers showing after the decimal.

11. What do you need to watch for when using the # sign for formatting?

That you don't create a situation like the example above where the number becomes 5. with the decimal but without any numbers after the decimal. It's better if you want a number to use a decimal place that at least one of the formatting symbols you put after the decimal is a zero instead of a pound sign.

12. If the value in Cell A1 is 4.235 and you use =TEXT(A1,"$#.##") & " per unit" what result will

you get?

$4.24 per unit

13. How can you take a date from Cell A1 and display its day of the week written fully? For example, Sunday.

=TEXT(A1,"dddd")

14. How can you display its abbreviated day of the week? For example, Sun.

=TEXT(A1,"ddd")

15. How can you isolate what day of the month it is from a date in Cell A1?

=TEXT(A1,"dd") or =TEXT(A1,"d") depending on whether you want a single-digit number or a two-digit number for the first days of the month.

16. How can you take a date from Cell A1 and display its month of the year written fully? For example, November.

=TEXT(A1,"mmmm")

17. How can you display its abbreviated month of the year? For example, Nov.

=TEXT(A1,"mmm")

18. How can you isolate the number for the month of the year from a date in Cell A1?

=TEXT(A1,"mm") or =TEXT(A1,"m") depending on whether you want a single-digit number or a two-digit number for the first months of the year.

19. How can you isolate the year from a date in Cell A1?

=TEXT(A1,"yy") or =TEXT(A1,"yyyy") depending on whether you want a two-digit or a four-digit year.

LIMITING ALLOWED INPUTS QUIZ ANSWERS

1. What is the issue that you run into if you let users enter data in any way they choose?

You can't easily analyze your data because of all of the variations in how people input the same information. One user might use USA, another might use U.S.A., another might use United States, and another might use U.S.. When you try to analyze data like that Excel (and most databases) will treat each of those values separately. It won't know that they all mean the same thing.

2. How can you get around this issue?

By limiting the answers that your users can provide. If you, for example, provide a dropdown list for users to choose from when entering Country, then you guarantee that only one value will be used for each country and that that data will be standardized.

3. What issue can you run into if you provide a dropdown menu of choices?

If you don't think through possible answers, you can

end up with a situation where users aren't able to provide the response they need to. For example, if you had a list of countries and you left Australia off the list and then had a customer from Australia, your users wouldn't be able to correctly list the customer's country.

4. What's one way around this?

Provide an Other category that includes a free-text option to capture those situations where your list of available inputs was missing a needed value and then monitor that list to add new values as needed to the main list.

5. What's one danger of doing this?

Users will use the Other category when they shouldn't and you are once more faced with data that should be grouped together that isn't because of poor data input.

6. How can you limit the values someone can input into a cell in Excel (general)?

Highlight the cells where you want to limit the input, click on Data Validation in the Data Tools section of the Data tab and then click on Data Validation again to bring up the Data Validation dialogue box and specify the limits you want.

7. If you want to limit users to a list of accepted text entries, what option should you choose? How do you specify the list?

Select the List option under Allow and then click into the Source box and highlight your list of accepted values. (It's best to have this be a list within the Excel worksheet, preferably on another worksheet that you then hide from users so that it's always available but can't be edited.)

8. If you want to limit users to only entering whole numbers, what option should you choose?

Whole Number.

9. If you want users to be able to enter a decimal number instead, what option should you choose?

Decimal.

10. When limiting a user's input to a number (either whole or decimal), what else do you need to do? And what should you be careful about when doing so?

Specify an accepted range of values that the user can enter. Think through possible values a user might need to enter. If you, for example, don't allow negative values or don't allow large enough values, this could restrict your users unnecessarily.

11. What will happen if you've applied data validation to a cell and a user tries to input an answer that isn't allowed?

Excel will generate an error message telling them that their entry isn't allowed.

12. Can you customize the message that displays? Where?

Yes. Under Error Alert.

13. How can you remove data validation from a set of cells?

Highlight the cells where you want to remove the data validation, go to the Data Tools section of the Data tab and click on Data Validation and then select Data Validation to bring up the Data Validation dialogue box, and choose Clear All in the bottom left corner.

LOCKING CELLS OR WORKSHEETS
QUIZ ANSWERS

1. Is it possible to keep users from editing the contents of cells in a worksheet? If so, how?

Yes. Select the range of cells that you want to lock from editing, right-click, choose Format Cells, and in the Format Cells dialogue box go to the Protection tab and choose Locked. Click OK. Next, go to the Cells section of the Home tab and click on Format and choose Protect Sheet from the dropdown menu. Provide a password to lock the worksheet and specify what users are allowed to do with locked cells.

You can also add protection to a worksheet or entire workbook using Protect Sheet or Protect Workbook under the Changes section of the Review tab.

2. What do you need to watch out for when locking a worksheet?

First, that you remember the password you used. Second, that you don't lock down so much that users can't use the worksheet. For example, if you lock column width and the values returned are large enough that the data displays as ####, that's not helpful to your users.

3. How can you remove protection from a worksheet?

Go back to the Format dropdown in the Cells section of the Home tab and choose Unprotect Sheet and provide your password. You can also remove protection from a worksheet or entire workbook using Protect Sheet or Protect Workbook under the Changes section of the Review tab.

4. Is it possible to hide the contents of cells in a worksheet as well? How?

Yes. Just click the Hidden box as well as the Locked box when you're protecting your cells.

HIDING A WORKSHEET
QUIZ ANSWERS

1. How can you hide a worksheet?

Right-click on the worksheet name and select Hide.

2. How can you unhide a worksheet?

Right-click on the name of any visible worksheet and choose Unhide. From there select from the dialogue box which worksheet(s) you want to unhide.

3. How can you hide a worksheet and keep someone from unhiding it?

Hide the worksheet and also protect the workbook. If the workbook has been locked then no one will be able to unhide the worksheet unless they have the password to remove protection from the workbook first.

TWO-VARIABLE ANALYSIS
GRID QUIZ ANSWERS

1. What does a two-variable analysis grid let you do?

It lets you create a table where you calculate possible outcomes given the values of two different variables. For example, hourly wage and hours worked to calculate amount earned for a week.

2. What shortcut can you use to make it easy to create a two-variable analysis grid?

Use the $ sign to fix your column and row references so that you only have to write the formula once and can then just copy and paste it to the rest of the table.

3. How can you combine a two-variable analysis grid with conditional formatting?

You can build the grid and then use conditional formatting to flag the results that meet your criteria. So, for example, if you need to earn $1,000 per week you can build a table with hourly wage and hours worked and then use conditional formatting to highlight in green all combinations where the amount earned is $1,000 or more.

MORE ANSWERS
QUIZ ANSWERS

1. What are three ways that you can find out more information on a topic from within Excel?

Hold your cursor over items in the menu section to see a description of what they do. Click on the Tell Me More option that's available under some of the menu items in Excel, such as Format Painter. Click on the question mark in the top right corner and search by subject.

2. What's the best way to find a function or learn more about a function you want to use?

Go to Insert Function under the Formulas tab and bring up the Insert Function dialogue box. Type in the function name that interests you or search by what you want to do. Once you have the function listed in the Select a Function box, click on it to see a brief description and format. If that's not enough, click on the Help on This Function link at the bottom of the dialogue box. You can also double-click on the function name to bring up the Function Arguments dialogue box which will give you a sample output and show how to build the function.

3. If you need more information than that, what options do you have outside of Excel?

Do an internet search and click on the support.office.com option. Look for user forums where your issue has already been discussed. Email me.

4. When is it better to use a forum than go to the Microsoft website?

When you need to know if it's possible to do something in Excel or want to know how to use a function for a specific purpose. The Microsoft website is good for functional questions but not is it possible type questions.

5. What's a nice trick you can use when troubleshooting a function?

Double-click on the cell that has the function in it and Excel will color-code the cell references in the formula as well as the actual cells being referred to by each cell reference. This can be a quick way to see that the wrong range of cells are being referenced by the formula or that ones that should be included aren't.

6. If you do something you didn't want to do, what's the easiest way to reverse it?

Ctrl + Z, Undo.

7. What's a best practice if you're building a really complex worksheet or one with lots of moving parts?

Save versions of the document so that if you do make a mistake you can't take back you don't lose all of your work. So solve one issue, save a copy, solve the next one, save a new copy, etc.

8. If you're using dates in your files names why use the YYYYMMDD format to record the date?

Because when you sort your file names, they'll sort in chronological order.

BONUS: EXERCISES

EXERCISE 1

Create a two-variable analysis grid that looks at home sale prices from $325,000 to $400,000 in increments of $25,000 and sales costs of 3%, 4%, 5%, and 6% with a mortgage balance due of $300,000.

Calculate what someone would net if they sold their property at each of those prices and sales costs given that mortgage balance? Apply conditional formatting so that all outcomes with a net of $32,500 or more are colored green.

EXERCISE 2

Starting with a grid like this one

	A	B	C	D	E	F
1	Sample A	Sample B	Sample C	Sample D	Sample E	Sample F
2	1	1	1	1	1	1
3	2	2	2	2	2	2
4	3	3	3	3	3	3
5	4	4	4	4	4	4
6	5	5	5	5	5	5
7	6	6	6	6	6	6
8	7	7	7	7	7	7
9	8	8	8	8	8	8
10	9	9	9	9	9	9
11	10	10	10	10	10	10

create the following conditional formats in Columns B
through F:

Sample B: No values visible but each cell is marked with
either an ex, an exclamation point, or a check mark based
upon its position within the range of values from 1 through

10. The first three with an ex, the next four with an exclamation mark, and the final three with a checkmark.

Sample C: The text for any cell that has a value between 5 and 7 is colored blue and bolded.

Sample D: Cells are filled with a solid bar of color that is bigger the larger the value, but all values below 2 are grouped together in the lowest range and all values 8 and up are grouped together in the highest range.

Sample E: Apply shaded color to the cells with the darkest color for the highest value. Customize the color to shade from light gold to dark gold.

Sample F: Apply a purple fill color and white font to the top 20% of the values in the range.

EXERCISE 3

Recreate the following table (formatting optional) and then provide answers to the questions below :

	A	B	C	D
1	**Customer**	**Date**	**Units**	**Product**
2	Jones	1/1/2018	5	Whatsit
3	Smith	1/2/2018	10	Whatsit
4	Baker	1/3/2018	25	Whatsit
5	Smith	1/4/2018	25	Thingy
6	Baker	1/5/2018	10	Thingy
7	Jones	1/6/2018	5	Thingy
8	Baker	1/7/2018	5	Whatsit
9	Jones	1/8/2018	5	Whatsit
10	Jones	1/9/2018	10	Whatsit
11				

1. How many total units has Customer Jones purchased?
2. How many Whatsits has Customer Baker purchased?
3. How many Thingies did Customer Smith purchase?

4. How many total units were purchased between January 1st and January 4th?

EXERCISE 4

Using the below data, create a stacked bar chart, a clustered column chart, and a line chart for the monthly entries and a pie chart using the YTD column.

For the line chart include a data table with legend keys and remove the legend.

For the bar chart change the default colors.

For the pie chart add labels that show the total value for each slice on the outside and explode the pie so that the slices are slightly separated.

	A	B	C	D	E	F	G	H
1		January	February	March	April	May	June	YTD
2	Alpha	15	20	25	30	35	40	165
3	Beta	25	23	21	19	17	15	120
4	Omega	10	20	10	20	10	20	90

EXERCISE 5

Using the same data from Exercise 3, isolate a list of your unique customer names and write a function that will sum the total number of units each customer bought. Assume your data covers thousands of rows and that you may be dealing with hundreds of customer names.

	A	B	C	D
1	**Customer**	**Date**	**Units**	**Product**
2	Jones	1/1/2018	5	Whatsit
3	Smith	1/2/2018	10	Whatsit
4	Baker	1/3/2018	25	Whatsit
5	Smith	1/4/2018	25	Thingy
6	Baker	1/5/2018	10	Thingy
7	Jones	1/6/2018	5	Thingy
8	Baker	1/7/2018	5	Whatsit
9	Jones	1/8/2018	5	Whatsit
10	Jones	1/9/2018	10	Whatsit
11				

BONUS:
EXERCISE ANSWERS

EXERCISE 1

Create a two-variable analysis grid that looks at home sale prices from $325,000 to $400,000 in increments of $25,000 and sales costs of 3%, 4%, 5%, and 6% with a mortgage balance due of $300,000.

Calculate what someone would net if they sold their property at each of those prices and sales costs given that mortgage balance? Apply conditional formatting so that all outcomes with a net of $32,500 or more are colored green.

* * *

There are multiple ways to create the above, but here is one way:

	A	B	C	D	E	F
1	Mortgage	$300,000				
2						
3				Sales Price		
4			$325,000	$350,000	$375,000	$400,000
5	Sale Cost	3%	$15,250	$39,500	$63,750	$88,000
6		4%	$12,000	$36,000	$60,000	$84,000
7		5%	$8,750	$32,500	$56,250	$80,000
8		6%	$5,500	$29,000	$52,500	$76,000

1. In Cell A1 type "Mortgage".

2. In Cell B1 type "$300,000".

3. In Cell C3 type "Sales Price".

4. In Cell C4 type "$325,000". In Cell D4 use the formula =C4+25000. Copy the formula from Cell D4 to Cells E4 through F4. Add a border and fill color to Cells C4 through F4.

5. Select Cells C3 through F3 and Merge & Center. Add a basic border and fill color to the newly created cell.

6. In Cell B5 type "3%". In Cell B6 use the formula =B5+.01. Copy the formula from Cell B6 to Cells B7 and B8. Add a border and fill color to Cells B5 through B8.

7. In Cell A5 type "Sale Cost".

8. Select Cells A5 through A8 and Merge & Center. Change the text orientation in the cell to Rotate Text Up. Add a border and fill color to the newly created cell. Middle Align the cell.

9. In Cell C5 add the formula =(C$4*(1-$B5))-$B$1. Copy the formula from Cell C5 to Cells C5 through F8. Add a border to Cells C5 through F8.

10. Select Cells C5 through F8 and apply Greater Than conditional formatting to the cells to color those with a value equal to or greater than $32,500 green.

EXERCISE 2

Starting with a grid like this one

	A	B	C	D	E	F
1	Sample A	Sample B	Sample C	Sample D	Sample E	Sample F
2	1	1	1	1	1	1
3	2	2	2	2	2	2
4	3	3	3	3	3	3
5	4	4	4	4	4	4
6	5	5	5	5	5	5
7	6	6	6	6	6	6
8	7	7	7	7	7	7
9	8	8	8	8	8	8
10	9	9	9	9	9	9
11	10	10	10	10	10	10

create the following conditional formats in Columns B through F:

Sample B: No values visible but each cell is marked with either an ex, an exclamation point, or a check mark based upon its position within the range of values from 1 through

10. The first three with an ex, the next four with an exclamation mark, and the final three with a checkmark.

Sample C: The text for any cell that has a value between 5 and 7 is colored blue and bolded.

Sample D: Cells are filled with a solid bar of color that is bigger the larger the value, but all values below 2 are grouped together in the lowest range and all values 8 and up are grouped together in the highest range.

Sample E: Apply shaded color to the cells with the darkest color for the highest value. Customize the color to shade from light gold to dark gold.

Sample F: Apply a purple fill color and white font to the top 20% of the values in the range.

* * *

	A	B	C	D	E	F
1	Sample A	Sample B	Sample C	Sample D	Sample E	Sample F
2	1	✖	1	1	1	1
3	2	✖	2	2	2	2
4	3	✖	3	3	3	3
5	4	❗	4	4	4	4
6	5	❗	5	5	5	5
7	6	❗	6	6	6	6
8	7	❗	7	7	7	7
9	8	✔	8	8	8	8
10	9	✔	9	9	9	9
11	10	✔	10	10	10	10

Sample B: Use Conditional Formatting, Icon Sets, Indicators, and choose the 3 Symbols (Uncircled) option.

Then go to Manage Rules, choose the rule and Edit Rule, and click on the box for Show Icon Only.

Sample C: Use Conditional Formatting, Highlight Cells Rules, Between, enter 5 and 7, and then choose Custom Format. Choose the Blue standard color and Bold formatting.

Sample D: Use Conditional Formatting, Data Bars, Solid Fill. Then go to Manage Rules, choose the rule and Edit Rule, and set the Minimum Type to Number and 2 and the Maximum Type to Number and 8.

Sample E: Use Conditional Formatting, Color Scales, Green-White Color Scale. Then go to Manage Rules, choose the rule and Edit Rule, and change the color under Minimum to a light gold color and the color under Maximum to a dark gold color.

Sample F: Use Conditional Formatting, Top/Bottom Rules, Top 10%, change it to 20%, and then choose Custom Format. Go to the Fill tab and choose the purple color. Go to the Font tab and change the color in the dropdown to white. Click OK.

EXERCISE 3

Recreate the following table (formatting optional) and then provide answers to the questions below :

	A	B	C	D
1	**Customer**	**Date**	**Units**	**Product**
2	Jones	1/1/2018	5	Whatsit
3	Smith	1/2/2018	10	Whatsit
4	Baker	1/3/2018	25	Whatsit
5	Smith	1/4/2018	25	Thingy
6	Baker	1/5/2018	10	Thingy
7	Jones	1/6/2018	5	Thingy
8	Baker	1/7/2018	5	Whatsit
9	Jones	1/8/2018	5	Whatsit
10	Jones	1/9/2018	10	Whatsit
11				

1. How many total units has Customer Jones purchased?
2. How many Whatsits has Customer Baker purchased?
3. How many Thingies did Customer Smith purchase?

4. How many total units were purchased between January 1st and January 4th?

* * *

The easiest way to answer most of these questions is to create a pivot table with Customer in the Rows section, Product in the Columns section, and Sum of Units in the Values section. To answer the last question, add Date to the Filters section and check only the boxes for January 1st through 4th.

	A	B	C	D
1	Date	(Multiple Items)		
2				
3	Sum of Units	Product		
4	Customer	Thingy	Whatsit	Grand Total
5	Baker		25	25
6	Jones		5	5
7	Smith	25	10	35
8	Grand Total	25	40	65

Drag fields between areas below:

▼ FILTERS	▦ COLUMNS
Date ▼	Product ▼

▦ ROWS	Σ VALUES
Customer ▼	Sum of Un... ▼

Answers:
1. 25
2. 30
3. 25
4. 65

* * *

Another option is to apply filters to the data. For question 1 you could filter by customer name and then highlight Column C to see the sum of the values, for example.

You could also sort the data by customer name and then product type for the first few questions.

EXERCISE 4

Using the below data, create a stacked bar chart, a clustered column chart, and a line chart for the monthly entries and a pie chart using the YTD column.

For the line chart include a data table with legend keys and remove the legend.

For the bar chart change the default colors.

For the pie chart add labels that show the total value for each slice on the outside and explode the pie so that the slices are slightly separated.

	A	B	C	D	E	F	G	H
1		January	February	March	April	May	June	YTD
2	Alpha	15	20	25	30	35	40	165
3	Beta	25	23	21	19	17	15	120
4	Omega	10	20	10	20	10	20	90

* * *

For the bar, column, and line chart options highlight Cells A1 through G4, go to the Charts section of the Insert tab, and choose the desired chart type from the dropdowns for each chart type.

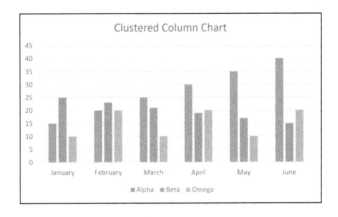

To add a data table and remove the legend from the line chart, click on the line chart and go to the Design tab under Chart Tools, click on Add Chart Element, and go to the Legend and Data Table options and make the appropriate selections.

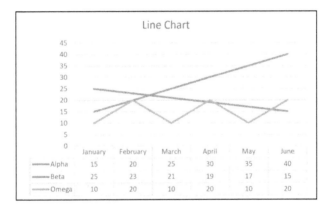

To change the colors in the bar chart, click on the chart. If Change Colors is available, you can choose from one of those options. Otherwise, click on each colored element in the chart, go to the Format tab under Chart Tools, and change the Shape Fill color for each one.

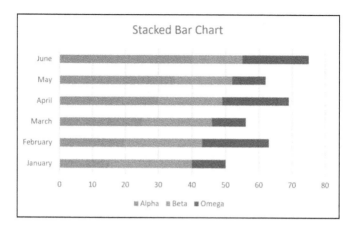

For the pie chart, highlight Cells A1 through A4 and H1 through H4, go to the Charts section of the Insert tab, and choose the 2-D pie chart option from the dropdowns for pie charts. To add labels to each slice, click on the chart and go to the Design tab under Chart Tools, click on Add Chart Element, and choose Data Labels and then Outside End. To explode the pie chart, click on the chart, go to Format Data Series on the right-hand side, click on Series Options at the top (the three bars), and explode the pie by about 7%.

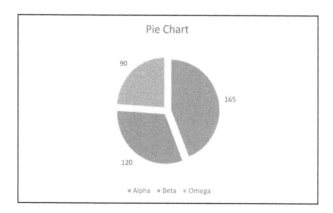

EXERCISE 5

Using the same data from Exercise 3, isolate a list of your unique customer names and write a function that will sum the total number of units each customer bought. Assume your data covers thousands of rows and that you may be dealing with hundreds of customer names.

	A	B	C	D
1	**Customer**	**Date**	**Units**	**Product**
2	Jones	1/1/2018	5	Whatsit
3	Smith	1/2/2018	10	Whatsit
4	Baker	1/3/2018	25	Whatsit
5	Smith	1/4/2018	25	Thingy
6	Baker	1/5/2018	10	Thingy
7	Jones	1/6/2018	5	Thingy
8	Baker	1/7/2018	5	Whatsit
9	Jones	1/8/2018	5	Whatsit
10	Jones	1/9/2018	10	Whatsit
11				

* * *

1. Copy your list of customer names from Column A to a new column that's separate from your existing data (in this case Column I) and remove duplicates from that column using Remove Duplicates from under the Data Tools section of the Data tab.

2. In the column next to that, in this case Column J, write a SUMIFS formula =SUMIFS(C:C,A:A,I2) which says to sum the number of units in Column C when the customer name in Column A is equal to the value in Cell I2 where the first of your list of unique customer names is.

3. Copy the SUMIFS formula from Cell J2 down as many rows as needed for all customer names in Column J.

The 100 Excel Functions Quiz Book

M.L. HUMPHREY

CONTENTS

INTRODUCTION

This is a companion book written to complement *50 Useful Excel Functions* and *50 More Excel Functions* by M.L. Humphrey and is geared towards those who are already familiar with the functions covered in those book who now want to test their knowledge through quizzes or to those who learn better from a question and answer format.

The quizzes in this book are in the same order as in *50 Useful Excel Functions* and then *50 More Excel Functions* but are sometimes grouped by related functions. So one quiz might cover, for example, functions related to date functions.

The first section of the book just has the questions, the next section of the book has the questions as well as the answers. There is also a bonus section that contains five exercises where you can test your knowledge of the various functions by applying them to specific real-life scenarios.

I encourage you to try to do each exercise first without looking at the solutions, since in the real world you'll be faced with a problem that needs solved and no one will be there to tell you which functions to use. However, I would also encourage you to have Excel open as you work each exercise so you can use the help functions within Excel to find the functions you need. Don't feel like you need to memorize every function in Excel in order to use it effectively. You just need to know what's possible and then what keywords or phrasing to use to help you find the right function.

Alright, then. Let's start with the first quiz.

QUIZZES

HOW FORMULAS AND
FUNCTIONS WORK QUIZ

1. If you're writing a basic formula in Excel, what symbols can you use to indicate this to Excel?

2. If you're starting a formula using a function in Excel, which symbol do you need to use to indicate this to Excel?

3. If you enter a formula in Excel and then hit enter, what are you going to see in that cell in your worksheet?

4. If you want to see the actual formula that's in a cell, how can you do that?

5. What is the difference between a formula and a function?

6. What are the symbols you can use for adding, subtracting, multiplying, or dividing in Excel?

7. What do the following formulas do?

    A. =3+2

    B. =3-2

    C. =3*2

    D. =3/2

    E. =4+(3*2)

    F. =(4+3)*2

8. What do the following formulas do?

    A. =A1+C1

    B. =A1-C1

    C. =A1*C1

    D. =A1/C1

    E. =E1+(A1*C1)

    F. =(E1+A1)*C1

9. What do examples E and F of the last two questions above demonstrate?

10. What's a best practice when building a really complex formula in Excel?

11. How do you write a function in Excel when it's at the beginning of a formula?

12. Can you use more than once function within a single cell in Excel?

13. What happens if you give the wrong cell range for your function?

WHERE TO FIND FUNCTIONS QUIZ

1. In newer versions of Excel where can you go to look for a function to perform a specific task?

2. What are the categories of functions available in Excel?

3. If you bring up the Insert Function dialogue box and are looking to perform a specific task with a function, where can you search for that?

4. What happens when you click on a function name under Select a Function in the Insert Function dialogue box?

5. If that's not enough information, what can you do?

6. What happens when you select a function from the Insert Function dialogue box?

7. If you already know the function you want to use, but aren't sure of the inputs or the order they need to be entered in, what can you do within your Excel worksheet?

8. If you click on the function name after you've typed, =FUNCTION_NAME(what will you get?

9. What if you still can't figure out what function to use to do what you want to do or don't even know if a function exists for what you're looking to do?

10. What can you do if you're using a version of Excel that's prior to Excel 2007 and so don't have a Formulas tab to go to but want to bring up the Insert Function dialogue box?

FORMULA AND FUNCTION BEST PRACTICES QUIZ

1. Name four best practices when working with formulas or functions.

2. Explain what it means to make your assumptions visible.

3. Explain what it means to use paste special-values when you're done with your calculations and when you should not do this.

4. How can you paste special-values to replace a formula with just the result of the formula?

5. Explain why you should store your raw data in one location and work on a copy of that data instead.

6. What's another best practice when doing a lot of complex work with a dataset that requires multiple steps and manipulations?

7. Why should you test your formulas before applying them to a large data set?

8. Why can't you just accept the results Excel gives you? Why should you always "gut check" those results?

COPYING FORMULAS QUIZ

1. What happens when you copy a formula from one cell to another?

2. If you write a formula and you want to fix the reference to a specific cell so that even if the formula is copied elsewhere it continues to reference that cell, how can you do this?

3. What if you just want to lock the row reference but not the entire cell reference?

4. What if you just want to lock the column reference but not the entire cell reference?

5. If you just want to move a formula to a new location without it changing, what's the best way to do that?

BASIC MATH FUNCTIONS QUIZ

1. What is the function you can use to sum a range of values or a range of cells?

2. How would you write a function to sum the values in Column A?

3. How would you write a function to sum the values in Rows 1 through 3?

4. How would you write a function to sum the values in Columns A, C, and E?

5. How would you write a function to sum the values in Cells A1 through B6?

6. How would you write a function to subtract the total of all customer orders in Column C from the amount collected which is listed in Cell F1?

7. What is the function you can use to multiply a range of values or a range of cells?

8. If you want to multiply number of units in Cell A1 times unit price in Cell B1 times tax rate in Cell C1, how would you write that using a function?

9. What is another way to do that that doesn't use a function?

10. What is the function you can use to multiply a range of values and then sum those results?

11. What are the inputs that go into that function?

12. If you have a table with number of units in Column A and unit price in Column B and you want to calculate the total earned (units times price and then summed across all rows), how would you write that using a single function?

13. What's another way to do that calculation?

14. When using SUMPRODUCT, what does the #VALUE! error message likely indicate?

15. What does Excel do with text entries that are included in a SUMPRODUCT cell range?

16. Can you use SUMPRODUCT for rows of data instead of columns?

17. Is there a function for subtracting values from one another?

18. Is there a function for dividing values by one another?

19. Why?

20. If you have a series of a hundred numbers in Column B that you want to subtract from the value in Cell A1, how can you use a function to do that?

AVERAGES, MEANS, AND MODES QUIZ

1. What is the difference between an average, a mean, and a mode?

2. What's a good idea when dealing with a large range of data points that will help you figure out whether average, mean, or mode works best for your data?

3. If I want to calculate the average of values in Cells A1 through A5, how can I do that using a function?

4. What happens if one of the cells in that range is blank?

5. What can you do to make sure that Excel includes all cells within the specified range when using the AVERAGE function?

6. What happens if one of the cells in that range contains text?

7. What can you do to make sure that Excel includes cells

with text in them when calculating an average over a range of cells?

8. Can you take an average of the returns of a TRUE/FALSE series of responses to get the overall percent of responses that were true? How?

9. If I have four cells with the values 2, 6, Other, and Now, what result will I get using AVERAGE? What result will I get using AVERAGEA?

10. How does AVERAGEA handle blank cells in a range?

11. How would you write the function to calculate the median of a range of values from Cells C1 through C9?

12. How does Excel calculate the median when there is an even number of values in the range?

13. Why can this be dangerous?

14. Can you use median with TRUE/FALSE values?

15. What's a way to work around the need to type the TRUE and FALSE into the function itself?

16. What function should you use to find the most common result when your data has a large bump that isn't near the midline?

17. How would you write this function for a range of values in Cells B2 through B10?

18. What does MODE.MULT let you do?

19. What is special about the MODE.MULT function?

20. How do you use MODE.MULT?

21. If you've properly used MODE.MULT, what will it look like in the formula bar when you click back into the cell for the function?

22. If you have multi-modal data where two values occur with the same high frequency but you use the MODE.SNGL or MODE function instead of the MODE.MULT function, what will happen?

23. What can you do if you want your MODE.MULT results to display in a row instead of in a column?

24. What is one issue with MODE.MULT that you're still going to run into?

25. How could you work around this issue?

MINIMUMS AND MAXIMUMS QUIZ

1. If you want the minimum value within a range, what function can you use to get it?

2. If you want the maximum value within a range, what function can you use to get it?

3. How would you write the function to calculate the minimum value in Column D?

4. How would you write the function to calculate the maximum value in Row 3?

5. What value will Excel return if you ask for the minimum or maximum of a range of values that have no numbers in them?

6. What will happen if you try to take the minimum or maximum of a range of values that has an error value in it such as #DIV/0!?

7. If you have a range of values that you want to take a minimum of but that range includes TRUE and FALSE

entries that you want included in the calculation, what function should you use?

8. How do MINA and MAXA treat TRUE or FALSE values?

9. How do MINA and MAXA treat text?

10. What result will you get from =MINA(A1:A3) where A1 is the word Other, A2 is 2, and A3 is 3?

11. What result will you get from =MINA(A1:A3) where A1 is -2, A2 is 2, and A3 is 3?

12. What result will you get from =MAXA(A1:A3) where A1 is -2, A2 is 2, and A3 is 3?

ROUNDING QUIZ

1. What functions can you use to round numbers?

2. If you want to round a number to a specified number of digits and it can either be rounded up or down depending on which number it's closest to, which function should you use?

3. If you want to round a number to a specified number of digits and you want to always round away from zero, which function should you use?

4. If you want to round a number to a specified number of digits and you want to always round towards zero, which function should you use?

5. What is the difference between using one of the rounding functions and just formatting a number to display a certain number of decimal places?

6. If you want to round the number 234.561 to the nearest whole number, how would you write that function?

7. What if you wanted to round it to one decimal place?

8. What if you wanted to round it to two decimal places?

9. What if you wanted to round it to the nearest 100's (so 200)?

10. If I tell Excel to round a number to the nearest four decimal places, but there are only two decimal places in the number now, what will Excel do?

11. How does Excel decide with the ROUND function whether to round up or to round down?

12. If you use the ROUNDUP function to round to the nearest two decimal places for 1.239, what will you get?

13. If you use the ROUNDDOWN function to round to the nearest two decimal places for 1.239, what will you get?

14. If you use the ROUNDUP function to round to the nearest two decimal places for 1.231, what will you get?

15. If you use the ROUNDDOWN function to round to the nearest two decimal places for 1.231, what will you get?

16. If you use the ROUNDUP function to round to the nearest two decimal places for -1.239, what will you get?

17. If you use the ROUNDDOWN function to round to the nearest two decimal places for -1.239, what will you get?

18. If you use the ROUNDUP function to round to the nearest two decimal places for -1.231, what will you get?

19. If you use the ROUNDDOWN function to round to the nearest two decimal places for -1.231, what will you get?

20. What issue can you run into if you use ROUNDUP or ROUNDDOWN instead of ROUND?

BASIC COUNT FUNCTIONS QUIZ

1. What does the COUNT function allow you to do?

2. Does COUNT include cells with text in them?

3. Does COUNT include cells with formulas in them that create a number or date?

4. Does COUNT include cells with formulas in them that create a text entry?

5. If a cell contains "1 unit" as its value, will COUNT count it?

6. How would you use COUNT on a range of cells from B2 through D8?

7. What function can you use if you also want to count cells that contain text in them?

8. What does this function allow you to do?

9. What happens when you have a function in a cell, say

=CONCATENATE(A1,B1,C1) but that cell is currently not displaying a value and you use each of the count functions?

10. What should you always do when using any function?

11. What does COUNTBLANK do?

12. If you have an issue with which cells are being counted by a specific count function, what should you do?

THE COUNTIFS, SUMIFS, AND AVERAGEIFS FUNCTIONS QUIZ

1. What is the difference between COUNTIFS, SUMIFS, and AVERAGEIFS?

2. If you have access to both COUNTIF and COUNTIFS (or both SUMIF and SUMIFS, or both AVERAGEIF and AVERAGEIFS), which one should you use? Why?

3. What is the difference between COUNTIF and COUNTIFS? What about SUMIF and SUMIFS? And AVERAGEIF and AVERAGEIFS?

4. If you want to count how many times the values in Cells C10 through C25 are the same as the value in Cell A1, how would you write that function?

5. What if you wanted to count how many times the cells in that range had text that included an e in it?

6. Could you count how many cells from Cells C10 through C25 have the same values as Cell A1 AND how

many have an e in them? If so, how would you write that and what issue would you potentially run into?

7. If you want to count how many times the values in Cells C10 through C25 are greater than the value in Cell A1, how would you write that?

8. If you want to count how many customers are from Alaska and have bought Widgets when your customer location is stored in Column C and your product is stored in Column E, how would you write that?

9. If you want to count how many customers have bought more than 10 of your product and are from Hawaii when customer location is stored in Column C and number of units is in Column D, how would you write that?

10. If you want to count how many times Student A scored over 90 and Student B scored over 90 when their test scores are recorded in Rows 2 and 3, how would you do that?

11. What do you need to watch out for when using COUNTIFS, SUMIFS, and AVERAGEIFS?

12. If you want to total the value of all customer orders, which is listed in Column H, for all customers from Maine, which is listed in Column C, and who bought Widgets, which is listed in Column E, how would you do that?

13. Can you total the value of all customer orders over $100 using SUMIF or SUMIFS? How would you write that assuming customer order value is listed in Column H?

14. What do the asterisk (*), the question mark (?), and the tilde (~) represent when you're writing a count, sum, or average criteria?

15. Can you calculate the average customer order for a customer in Colorado who made a purchase in June, assuming that customer order is stored in Column H, customer location is in Column C, and purchase month is in Column B? How would you write that?

16. If there are no customer transactions that meet that criteria what result is Excel going to return?

17. With COUNTIFS, SUMIFS, and AVERAGEIFS, if you have three criteria you specify and two of the three are met, what will happen with that entry?

18. Why is this important?

BASIC TEXT
FUNCTIONS QUIZ

1. If you want to convert a text string into uppercase letters, which function should you use?

2. What if you want to convert a text string into lowercase letters?

3. What if you want the initial letter of each word to be capitalized, but the rest to be in lowercase?

4. Let's say that you have a text string in Cell C10 and another in Cell C11 and that you want to combine those entries with a space between them and convert them into uppercase letters. How could you do that?

5. What does CONCATENATE do?

6. What is the difference between proper case and title case?

7. What does the LEFT function do?

8. If you want to return the first five characters of the text in Cell A1, how would you do that?

9. Does this function work with numbers as well?

10. What happens if the number of characters you specify is greater than the number of characters in the string you reference?

11. What happens if you don't specify a number of characters to return?

12. For languages that don't work with characters, like Chinese, Japanese, and Korean, which function will do the same for those languages?

13. If you want to return the last two characters of a text string, how can you do that?

14. What does the MID function do?

15. What happens if the start point you provide for the MID function is greater than the number of characters in the string?

16. What happens if you use MID and ask Excel to return more characters than there are in the text string?

17. What other function could you use to get the same result as =MID(A1,1,2)?

18. If you want to take a text string and remove all spaces from it except for one space between each word, which function can you use to do that?

19. If you had a list of entries with first name, middle name, and last name in separate columns, Columns A, B,

and C, and you wanted to combine those entries for each row into one entry with only one space between each word, and you knew that not every entry had a middle name, how could you use two functions to do that in one cell? Write the function for Row 1.

20. What do you need to be careful of when using any of the above functions? What can you do when you're done with your manipulation to address this?

21. What type of inputs will CONCATENATE accept? And how do they need to be written?

22. If you want there to be a space or a comma in your final CONCATENATE result, how do you do that?

23. With CONCATENATE if you get a NAME#? error, what has generally gone wrong?

24. What function is Excel replacing CONCATENATE with?

THE TEXT FUNCTION QUIZ

1. What does Excel say that the TEXT function can do?

2. What else can the TEXT function actually do?

3. If you have a date in Cell A1 and want to pull the full name of the day of the week, how would you do that using the TEXT function?

4. What about the month of the year?

5. If you use TEXT to create number formats, for example =TEXT(A1,"$0.00"), what issue can you run into?

6. What is the other thing to be aware of when using the TEXT function with a number?

7. What's one quick way to see valid number formats you can use with the TEXT function?

8. If you wanted to return the number value in Cell A1 as "50% Win Rate", how could you do that using TEXT?

THE TODAY AND NOW
FUNCTIONS QUIZ

1. What does the TODAY function do?

2. How do you write it?

3. Why would you use it?

4. If you wanted to calculate how many days it's been since someone purchased your product, which is the better option: have a cell that uses =TODAY() and then another cell that calculates days since purchase or just have a cell that calculates days since purchase and incorporates TODAY() into the formula? Why?

5. What does the NOW function do?

6. What's the difference between using TODAY and NOW?

7. Why does this matter?

8. What do you need to be aware of when using both TODAY and NOW?

9. How does Excel treat dates for the purpose of addition and subtraction?

10. So if you wanted to calculate the date five and a half days from today's date, what could you use?

11. What if you wanted to calculate the date and time exactly five and a half days from this moment?

12. Is it possible that those two formulas could return different dates?

THE IF FUNCTION QUIZ

1. What does an IF function do?

2. Translate the IF function =IF(A2>25,0,A2*0.05) into a written description.

3. What is another way to think about the components of an IF function?

4. What does it mean that you can nest IF functions?

5. If you're going to nest IF functions, which is it better to replace, the Then portion or the Else portion? Why?

6. Translate the IF function =IF(A9>$A$5,$B$5,IF(A9> $A$4,$B$4,0)) into a written description.

7. If you were to copy the above formula into a new cell, how would it change?

8. If you have a long and complex nested IF function that you can't get to work, what are some ways you can troubleshoot the IF function to figure out what's wrong?

9. What is the most likely issue if Excel tells you you've entered too many arguments with an IF function?

10. What should you always do with an IF function that you create? (Or any function really?)

11. If you write an IF function that's referencing a table of fixed values (like a discount table) what should you always be sure to do?

VLOOKUP QUIZ

1. What does VLOOKUP do?

2. What must you do if you're using VLOOKUP on a table?

3. What's the best use for VLOOKUP?

4. Do the values in a reference table need to be an exact match for the value you're looking for for VLOOKUP to work?

5. What is the minimum number of columns your data needs for VLOOKUP to work?

6. Can the column that has the values you're looking up be located anywhere in your data?

7. How do you tell Excel whether to look for an exact match or an approximate match?

8. What is the difference between an exact match and an approximate match?

9. What is =VLOOKUP(25,A1:E10,3,FALSE) saying to do?

10. What is =VLOOKUP(25,A1:E10,2,TRUE) saying to do?

11. What do you need to be careful of when using VLOOKUP with apparent numbers or dates?

12. What should you always do when using any function in Excel?

THE AND & OR FUNCTIONS QUIZ

1. What does the AND function do?

2. What does the OR function do?

3. What is =AND(A1>5,A2>4) asking?

4. What is =OR(A1>5,A2>4) asking?

5. What is =AND(A1>B1,A2>B2) asking?

6. What is =IF(AND(A1="Jones",B1="Whatsit"),C1,D1) doing?

7. What is =IF(OR(A1="Canton",B1="Toledo"),G1,G1*2) doing?

THE TRUE, FALSE AND NA
FUNCTIONS QUIZ

1. What do the TRUE and FALSE functions do?

2. When might you use them?

3. What does the NA function do?

4. When might you use the NA function?

5. What do you need to remember when using the TRUE, FALSE, or NA functions?

RANDOM NUMBERS QUIZ

1. What function will return a random number greater than or equal to 0 and less than 1 evenly distributed?

2. What function will return a random whole number between two values you specify?

3. If I want to return any possible value, including a decimal value between 0 and 100, how can I do that?

4. If I want to return any whole number between 0 and 100, how can I do that?

5. What do you need to be careful of when using either function?

6. How can you work around this if you need to capture that value?

RANKING QUIZ

1. What function or functions can you use if you want to know the rank of a specific value within a range of possible values? In other words, is this the 5th largest number, the 10th, the 20th, etc. compared to other numbers in the range?

2. If you want to know the rank of a value in Cell A1 from within the range of Cells A1 through A15, how can you write that function using ascending values?

3. What about using descending values?

4. To use the functions does your data have to be sorted?

5. What happens if you use RANK on a data set where there are multiples of a value?

6. How do RANK.EQ and RANK.AVG differ?

THE SMALL AND LARGE
FUNCTIONS QUIZ

1. What does the SMALL function do?

2. What does the LARGE function do?

3. Can you technically use SMALL to return the largest value in a range and LARGE to return the smallest value in a range?

4. What does the ROWS function do?

THE IFNA AND
IFERROR QUIZ

1. What function can you use to suppress an #N/A! result in a formula?

2. Apply that function to the following formula: =VLOOKUP(D:D,'Advertising Spend By Series'!E:F,2, FALSE) so that a value of 0 is returned instead of the #N/A! error message.

3. Now apply the function to the following formula: =VLOOKUP(D:D,'Advertising Spend By Series'!E:F, FALSE)so that a value of "No Match" is returned instead of the #N/A! error message.

4. And also apply the function to the following formula: =VLOOKUP(D:D,'Advertising Spend By Series'!E:F,2, FALSE) so that a blank value is returned instead of the #N/A! error message.

5. What function can you use to suppress all error messages instead of just #N/A!?

6. Apply that function to a situation where you are dividing the value in Cell A1 by the value in Cell B1 and you want to return a blank result instead of an error message.

7. Now apply that function to a situation where you are dividing the value in Cell A1 by the value in Cell B1 and you want to return a value of "Error" instead of a specific error message.

8. What is the danger in using IFNA or IFERROR?

9. What is one way of addressing this issue?

THE NOT
FUNCTION QUIZ

1. What functions is the NOT function related to?

2. Why do I encourage you to find a way to use a function other than the NOT function to build a formula?

3. What result will you get if you use =NOT(FALSE)?

4. What result will you get if you use =NOT(TRUE)?

5. How could you use the NOT function?

6. Take the formula =NOT(B5<12). What value will it return if the value in Cell B5 is 2? What about if it's 14?

7. How could you evaluate that condition (whether B5 is less than 12 or equal to or greater than 12) with an IF function and get the same result as using the NOT function above?

THE HLOOKUP
FUNCTION QUIZ

1. What function is the HLOOKUP function related to?

2. What does HLOOKUP do?

3. What will this formula do:
   =HLOOKUP("April",B1:M12,4,FALSE)

4. What can you look up using HLOOKUP?

5. If you look up a text string, what do you need to be sure to do?

6. What are wildcards and how can you use them when looking up text?

7. In the table you're going to search using HLOOKUP, where do the values you're searching for need to be?

8. In the table you're going to search using HLOOKUP, where do the values you want to return need to be?

9. What is the difference between using FALSE and TRUE as the final input to the HLOOKUP function?

10. What is the risk to using TRUE as the third input to the HLOOKUP function?

11. Can you sort the values in a row in ascending order?

12. When you tell Excel which row to pull your result from using HLOOKUP, what number do you need to provide? Is it the Row number in the worksheet or something else?

13. If you provide a row value of 1 in the HLOOKUP function what will that return?

14. If you ask HLOOKUP to find an exact match and there isn't one, what value will Excel return?

15. What could potentially result in an incorrect error message when using HLOOKUP?

THE TRANSPOSE
FUNCTION QUIZ

1. What does the TRANSPOSE function do?

2. Does TRANSPOSE work on a table of values that covers multiple rows and/or columns?

3. What do you have to do special because TRANSPOSE is an array formula?

4. If you want to take the values in Cells C1 through C5 and place them in Cells E8 through I8, how would you do that?

5. If all you want to do is change the orientation of your data, what is a better option?

6. What benefit does the TRANSPOSE function give over doing that?

THE INDEX
FUNCTION QUIZ

1. What are the two tasks that the INDEX function can perform?

2. What is the following formula supposed to do:
=INDEX(A2:E7,3,4)

3. Does the INDEX function require you to include a header row or row labels in the specified cell range?

4. How do you determine the row number value to use in the INDEX function?

5. How do you determine the column number value to use in the INDEX function?

6. Can you use the INDEX function with more than one table of data? How?

7. What happens if you use the fourth variable in the INDEX function without providing multiple table range values in the first variable?

8. If you want to use the INDEX function to pull an entire column or row of data, what do you need to do?

9. Can you easily copy and paste an array formula?

10. Once you've extracted values from a table using the INDEX function are the results fixed values?

THE MATCH
FUNCTION QUIZ

1. What does the MATCH function do?

2. If the MATCH function returns a value of 2 for the following formula, what does that mean:
$$=MATCH(\$A12,\$A\$2:\$A\$7,0)$$

3. What is the value in using the MATCH function?

4. What kinds of values can MATCH look for?

5. What are the three match types that you can use with MATCH?

6. If you're not looking for an exact match what do you need to do first? And how will your choice of match type impact this?

7. What is the default match type used by MATCH? Why is this a problem?

8. Is the value returned by MATCH the row number or the column number in the worksheet or something else?

TEXT FUNCTIONS
QUIZ

1. What does the LEN function do?

2. What does the SEARCH function do?

3. What does the FIND function do?

4. So what is the difference between SEARCH and FIND?

5. If you're working in a language such as Japanese, Chinese, or Korean that uses bytes instead of characters what functions should you use instead of LEN, SEARCH, and FIND?

6. What does the EXACT function do?

7. Is EXACT case-sensitive?

8. What result would LEN return for =LEN("This one")? Why?

9. Can you use LEN with a cell reference, so for example, =LEN(D10)?

10. How does LEN handle a formula in a cell?

11. What is the following formula doing:
    =LEFT(A1,LEN(A1)-LEN(" units"))?

12. How could you accomplish the same task using the SEARCH function? Explain why this works.

13. Do you have to start at the beginning of a text string if using the SEARCH or FIND functions?

14. If you do use the third input in the SEARCH or FIND function, what do you need to keep in mind about the value that's returned?

15. What will your result be if the value you search for using SEARCH or FIND isn't in that text string?

16. What will your result be if the start position you provide is a negative number or a larger number than the length of the text string in SEARCH or FIND?

17. What values will =SEARCH("coz*","teacozy") and =FIND("coz*","teacozy") return? Why?

18. What values will =SEARCH("t","Teapot") and =FIND("t","Teapot") return? Why?

19. Does EXACT look for differences in formatting between two entries?

20. If you wanted to compare the values in Cells A1 and D2, how would you write that using the EXACT function? What value would you expect if the two values were equal?

What would you expect if they were not?

21. If you use EXACT with two cells that use different formulas but return the same numeric value, what will the result be?

THE CONVERT FUNCTION
QUIZ

1. What does the CONVERT function do?

2. Name three types of conversions CONVERT can do:

3. What happens if you use units from two different categories in the same CONVERT function?

4. Are the units used in the CONVERT function case-sensitive?

5. Write the formula for converting 57 degrees Fahrenheit to Celsius:

6. Write the formula for determining how many days there are in five years using the CONVERT function:

7. Give a likely explanation for why the value returned in the last example is a decimal:

8. Write the formula for converting 60 miles to kilometers.

NUMERIC FUNCTIONS QUIZ

1. What function would you use to take the absolute value of a number?

2. Write the function for the absolute value of -3:

3. What does the MOD function do?

4. What does the QUOTIENT function do?

5. Can you use the MOD and QUOTIENT functions to take a decimal number, such as 12.345 and separate the integer portion from the decimal portion? If so, how?

6. What is another function that allows you to extract just the integer portion of a number?

7. Apply this function to 12.345 to get 12:

8. What is the difference between truncating a number and rounding a number?

9. How would you truncate 12,543 to the nearest 1000s?

10. Is this the same value you'd get if you rounded to the nearest 1000s?

11. How does the INT function differ from the ROUND and TRUNC functions?

12. How would you use the TRUNC function (and perhaps another function) to separate the number -12.345 into its integer and decimal components?

POWERS AND SQUARE
ROOTS QUIZ

1. What does it mean to raise a number to a power?

2. What function can be used to do this?

3. Is there a way to do this with notation instead? How?

4. Show how to take 5 to the power of 4 using both the function and the notation method.

5. Can you use both of these methods to take a root power, such as the square root of a number? If so, write how to take the square root of 9.

6. Is there a function that will specifically let you take the square root of a number? What is it? Apply it to 9.

7. What is the function that will let you return the value of Pi to fifteen digits?

8. How would you write that?

9. How would you calculate the area of a circle (which is Pi times the square of the radius) using the above functions where the radius is 3?

10. What does the function SQRTPI give you?

11. If you wanted the square root of Pi itself, how could you get that value?

LOGARITHMS QUIZ

1. What formula would you use to obtain the value of e?

2. What does the function used in the prior question do?

3. What is =LOG(100) asking?

4. Write a formula that uses the LOG function to determine what power you'd have to take the number 2 to get a result of 24:

5. Write a formula that uses the LOG function to determine what power you'd have to take e to to get a result of 24:

6. Write a formula that uses the LN function to make the same determination:

7. What does the LN function do?

8. What does the LOG function do?

9. Which of the two is more flexible?

10. What does the LOG10 function do?

11. Should you use it?

FACTORIALS AND
COMBINATIONS QUIZ

1. What is the difference between permutations and combinations?

2. What does a factorial do?

3. What function in Excel will do this calculation for you?

4. What formula would you write to determine the number of possible permutations for a group of ten people?

5. What happens with the FACT function if you input a decimal value, for example =FACT(3.95)?

6. What value will Excel return if you ask for the factorial of zero?

7. What happens if you ask for the factorial of a negative number?

8. If you had a group of ten individuals and wanted to give out first, second, and third place medals, how would you use the FACT function to calculate the number of possible three-person outcomes?

9. What if you instead wanted to calculate the number of three-person teams that could be built out of a population of nine people. What function would you use?

10. What does this function do?

11. How would you use it to calculate the number of two-person teams possible in a group of four individuals?

12. What function would you use if you want to know the number of possible combinations where each possibility can be chosen multiple times? (In other words, you can have 22 as an outcome.)

13. So if you had a raffle drawing and there were ten people participating, each with one ticket and where each ticket was put back into the draw each time, and you wanted to know the odds of one person winning all three draws how would you do that calculation?

PRESENT AND FUTURE
VALUES QUIZ

1. If you want to know the current value of a series of identical payments that you'll receive on an annual basis in the future, what function can you use to calculate that?

2. What are the inputs to this function?

3. What does the NPV function do?

4. What is the advantage of the NPV function over the PV function?

5. What limitation do both PV and NPV share?

6. If I have a range of values in Cells B2 through B8 that represent annual payments that I'm going to receive starting one year from now and want to calculate the net present value of those amounts using a ten percent annual interest rate, how would I write that:

7. What if I'm going to receive $1,000 each year for the next five years and the annual interest rate is 10%. What formula would you write to calculate the current value of those future payments?

8. What does the FORECAST function do?

9. Why is it important to remember that it only works with a linear trend?

10. Because of this, what should you do before using the FORECAST function?

11. What are the order of the inputs to the FORECAST function?

12. Can you use FORECAST to predict a value prior to your data range? In other words, what y would be at a smaller value of x than is shown in your data table?

THE FREQUENCY
FUNCTION QUIZ

1. What does the FREQUENCY function do?

2. What must you have in order to use the FREQUENCY function?

3. What does it mean that FREQUENCY is an array function?

4. What are the inputs to the FREQUENCY function?

5. How is a bins array entry structured? And how is it used by Excel?

6. What is an easy way to get a list of bin array values that correspond to all potential values in your data set?

7. If the range of values you want to evaluate are in Column C and your bins values are in Cells D2 through D6, how would you write the formula to calculate your frequencies for each of those bin values?

THE HOW EXCEL HANDLES
DATES QUIZ

1. By default what does the number 1 represent with respect to a date in Excel?

2. Can Excel handle dates prior to 1900?

3. Can you use addition and subtraction with dates in Excel? Why or why not?

4. What is a serial_number with respect to date functions in Excel?

5. How does Excel handle dates differently on the Mac operating system? What does this mean for someone working between a PC and a Mac using Excel?

6. How does Excel account for this?

7. If you enter a two-digit year, for example '29, how will Excel treat that in terms of the century it applies?

DATE FUNCTIONS
QUIZ

1. What does the DATE function do?

2. What happens if you use the DATE function with a date prior to January 1, 1900, so for example if you use =DATE(1880,1,1)?

3. Can you use a value for the month portion of the DATE function that is greater than 12? What about less than 1?

4. What about days of the month? Can you have a number greater than 31 or a negative number?

5. Write a formula that takes a date stored in Cell B2 and adds four months to it.

6. What does the YEAR function do?

7. How would you use YEAR to extract the year portion of the date March 1, 2010?

8. What happens if you fail to use quotation marks around a date used in a YEAR function?

9. What does the MONTH function do?

10. What result will you get from =MONTH("April, 1, 1952")?

11. What does the DAY function do?

12. What does the HOUR function do?

13. What will =HOUR(NOW()) give you?

14. Since Excel treats dates as numbers, what is the value of an hour under Excel's system?

15. Will you get a result with =HOUR(.166667)?

16. How does the MINUTE function work?

17. Since Excel treats dates as numbers, what is the value of a minute under Excel's system?

18. What does the SECOND function do?

19. What result will you get from
                    =SECOND("12:32:21")?

20. Since Excel treats dates as numbers, what is the value of a second under Excel's system?

21. If you enter a date without entering a specific time of day and then use the HOUR, MINUTE, or SECOND function on that date, what value will Excel give you?

22. What does the WEEKDAY function do?

23. What is the default setting for the WEEKDAY function in terms of numbering the days of the week?

24. If August 13, 2019 is a Tuesday and I use =WEEKDAY("August 13, 2019") what value will I get back?

25. What portion of the WEEKDAY function should you change if you want the numbers returned to map to different days of the week? How would you change the above formula so that Monday is treated as a 1 and Tuesday returns a value of 2 instead?

26. What does the following formula do:
       =IF(WEEKDAY(A1,2)>5,12.95,9.95)

27. What does the WEEKNUM function do?

28. How does Excel define a week for purposes of the WEEKNUM function?

29. How do you get Excel to define a week in accordance with ISO standards when using the WEEKNUM function? And how does it work?

30. What is another function you can use to get Excel to apply the ISO standard when determining the week number? And when did it become available?

DATE CALCULATION FUNCTIONS IN EXCEL QUIZ

1. What does the DAYS function do?

2. Do you need the DAYS function to do this?

3. What does the DAYS360 function do?

4. Are there different methods with DAYS360 for handling the last day of the month when it's either in February or in a month with 31 days?

5. What does the EDATE function do?

6. What is another way to get this same result?

7. If I use =EDATE("March 1, 2019",4) what result will that give me?

8. How does EDATE handle partial month values, such as =EDATE("March 1, 2019",4.9)?

9. What does the EOMONTH function do?

10. What do you need to do with the result of an EDATE or EOMONTH formula?

WORKDAYS AND NETWORKDAYS QUIZ

1. What does the NETWORKDAYS function do?

2. How is this different from just using the DAYS function?

3. How can you incorporate holidays into the NETWORKDAYS function?

4. What if you don't want NETWORKDAYS to include the start date and the end date in the calculation?

5. Using NETWORKDAYS write a formula calculating the number of workdays between August 28, 2019 and September 4, 2019 where September 2, 2019 is a holiday and you don't want to count the first or the last day in the count:

6. What function would you use to calculate workdays if your weekend days are not Saturday and Sunday?

7. With which version of Excel did this function become available?

8. Explain what the weekend input to the NETWORKDAYS.INTL function does:

9. Are NETWORKDAYS and NETWORKDAYS.INTL directly interchangeable? Can you just change one to the other and have it work?

10. What does the WORKDAY function do?

11. Does WORKDAY include the start date in its count like NETWORKDAYS does?

12. What does the WORKDAY.INTL function do?

13. Let's say that your team is working six-day weeks and that they're allowed to have Wednesdays off. It's currently August 23, 2019 and your team says they need twelve more days to finish the project. There is a holiday on September 2, 2019. When will they complete the project?

14. What if they tell you this on the morning of the 23rd and you know that they'll be working all day so it will count towards their timeline. Will this impact the completion date?

15. Can you create a custom set of off days using the WORKDAY.INTL function? How?

COMBINING FUNCTIONS QUIZ

1. Is it possible to write a formula that uses more than one function?

2. How would you write a formula that returns a value of TRUE if the value in Cell A1 is greater than 10 or the value in Cell B1 is greater than 10 and a value of FALSE otherwise?

3. What do you need to be careful about when combining functions together in one formula?

4. Do you need to use an equals sign in front of each function name when you combine functions in a single formula?

5. What should you explore further if you're running into file size issues because of repeat calculations in your Excel worksheet?

WHEN THINGS GO
WRONG QUIZ

1. Name five different error messages you might see.

2. What does #REF! generally indicate?

3. How can you see where the cell that was deleted was located in your formula?

4. What does a #VALUE! message indicate?

5. What does a #DIV/0! message indicate?

6. If the #DIV/0! message is legitimate because nothing has been entered yet, what's a quick way to suppress it?

7. What does a #N/A error message generally mean?

8. What can you check for if this happens and you don't think it should have?

9. What does the IFERROR function do? What do you need to be careful with if you use it?

10. What does the #NUM! error message generally indicate?

11. What is a circular reference?

12. If you don't think you have a circular reference but Excel tells you you do, what should you check for?

13. If you're trying to figure out what cells are feeding the value in a cell where can you go to do that?

14. If Excel tells you you have too few arguments, what should you check for?

15. What can you do with a formula that just isn't working the way it should be?

CELL NOTATION QUIZ

1. What is Cell A1 referencing?

2. Name two ways you can reference more than one cell in a function.

3. Can you reference a cell in another worksheet?

4. Can you reference a cell in another workbook?

5. What's an easy way to reference a cell in another worksheet or workbook?

QUIZ ANSWERS

HOW FORMULAS AND FUNCTIONS
WORK QUIZ ANSWERS

1. If you're writing a basic formula in Excel, what symbols can you use to indicate this to Excel?

You can use a plus sign (+), a minus sign (-), or an equals sign (=).

2. If you're starting a formula using a function in Excel, which symbol do you need to use to indicate this to Excel?

The equals sign (=).

3. If you enter a formula in Excel and then hit enter, what are you going to see in that cell in your worksheet?

The result. So, for example, if you type =2+2 into a cell and hit enter you will see 4, the result of adding two plus two, in the cell where you entered the formula.

4. If you want to see the actual formula that's in a cell, how can you do that?

Click on the cell and look in the formula bar or double-click on the cell to see the formula in the cell itself.

5. What is the difference between a formula and a function?

A function lets you perform a specified task. It's like a programmed shortcut. That task can be mathematical (like SUM) or it can be related to text (like CONCATENATE), dates, or logic. A formula is a way of performing a calculation using Excel and it can not only involve functions but also just basic math notation.

6. What are the symbols you can use for adding, subtracting, multiplying, or dividing in Excel?

To add you can use the plus sign (+). To subtract you can use the minus sign (-). To multiply you can use the asterisk (*). And to divide you can use the forward slash (/).

7. What do the following formulas do?

 A. =3+2
  Adds 3 to 2

 B. =3-2
  Subtracts 2 from 3

 C. =3*2
  Multiplies 3 by 2

 D. =3/2
  Divides 3 by 2

 E. =4+(3*2)
  Multiplies 3 by 2 and then adds the result to 4

 F. =(4+3)*2
  Adds 4 to 3 and then multiplies the result by 2

8. What do the following formulas do?

 A. =A1+C1
  Adds the value in A1 to the value in C1

B. =A1-C1

Subtracts the value in C1 from the value in A1

C. =A1*C1

Multiplies the value in A1 by the value in C1

D. =A1/C1

Divides the value in A1 by the value in C1

E. =E1+(A1*C1)

Multiplies the value in A1 by the value in C1 and then adds the result to the value in E1

F. =(E1+A1)*C1

Adds the value in E1 to the value in A1 and then multiplies the result by the value in C1

9. What do examples E and F from the last two questions above demonstrate?

How important it is when writing a complex formula that you place your parens in the right place, because that will determine the order in which Excel performs its calculations and will impact your answer.

10. What's a best practice when building a really complex formula in Excel?

Build it in pieces and test that each piece is calculating correctly before combining all of the pieces together.

11. How do you write a function in Excel when it's at the beginning of a formula?

=FUNCTION_NAME(

You start with an equals sign, follow that with the function name, and then immediately follow that with an opening paren.

12. Can you use more than once function within a single cell in Excel?

Yes.

13. What happens if you give the wrong cell range for your function?

Garbage in, garbage out. It won't do what you want it to do. For a function to properly work it needs to be the right one and you need to give it the right inputs in the right order.

WHERE TO FIND FUNCTIONS
QUIZ ANSWERS

1. In newer versions of Excel where can you go to look for a function to perform a specific task?

The Formulas tab will show you a Function Library set of dropdowns arranged by type (Financial, Logical, Text, etc.) and you can hold your mouse over each one for a brief description of what it does. But if you don't know the function you want, it's better to go to Insert Function and bring up the Insert Function dialogue box. This will let you search using a few keywords for the function you want.

2. What are the categories of functions available in Excel?

Financial, Logical, Text, Date & Time, Lookup & Reference, Math & Trig, Statistical, Engineering, Cube, Information, Compatibility, Web

3. If you bring up the Insert Function dialogue box and are looking to perform a specific task with a function, where can you search for that?

In the Search For a Function box at the top. Enter a few keywords related to what you want to do and then click on Go. Excel will list functions in the Select a Function box that meet those keywords.

4. What happens when you click on a function name under Select a Function in the Insert Function dialogue box?

Excel will show you a brief description of what the function does as well as a sample of what inputs the function requires to work.

5. If that's not enough information, what can you do?

Click on Help on This Function in the bottom left corner.

6. What happens when you select a function from the Insert Function dialogue box?

It brings up the Function Arguments box which will show you the description for the function, a sample output for the function based upon the choices you make, and input boxes for you to add the information required for the function.

7. If you already know the function you want to use, but aren't sure of the inputs or the order they need to be entered in, what can you do within your Excel worksheet?

Type =FUNCTION_NAME to see the Excel description of what the function does. Type =FUNCTION_NAME(to see a list of the inputs for the function and the order in which they need to appear.

8. If you click on the function name after you've typed, =FUNCTION_NAME(what will you get?

An Excel Help dialogue box for that function.

9. What if you still can't figure out what function to use to do what you want to do or don't even know if a

function exists for what you're looking to do?

Do an internet search. Chances are someone else at some point wanted to do the exact same thing you do.

10. What can you do if you're using a version of Excel that's prior to Excel 2007 and so don't have a Formulas tab to go to but want to bring up the Insert Function dialogue box?

Type an equals sign into a cell, go to the white dropdown box to the left of the formula bar, click on the dropdown arrow, and choose More Functions from the bottom of the list.

FORMULA AND FUNCTION BEST PRACTICES QUIZ ANSWERS

1. Name four best practices when working with formulas or functions.

Make your assumptions visible, use paste special-values when you're done with your calculations, store your raw data in one location and work on a copy of that data for any calculations or manipulations, test your formulas to make sure they work under all possible circumstances especially threshold cases.

2. Explain what it means to make your assumptions visible.

While it's possible to write a formula that has all of the information written within a cell, it's better to show on your worksheet any inputs into that formula. For example, if I assume that selling my house is going to cost me 3% in realtor fees, it's better to have a field in Excel for realtor fees that I can see at a glance and to reference that cell with my formula than to build that 3% amount into a formula where I'll only see it if I click on that cell. (Especially since that number is very likely wrong.)

3. Explain what it means to use paste special-values when you're done with your calculations and when you should not do this.

Do not do this if you expect to update your information that's feeding the calculation. This should only be done when you are completely finished with your analysis. Because if you do it and then update an input into the formula, the formula no longer exists and your final answer will not update with the new information.

But the reason to do this is the same. If you've finished your calculation using paste special-values will lock in your results so that they can't be impacted by deleting data that was used to make the calculation.

4. How can you paste special-values to replace a formula with just the result of the formula?

Click on the cell with formula and Copy (Ctrl +C is the easiest way to do this), right-click on the same cell, and choose to Paste Special and then the Values option from the dropdown menu. (It's the one with the 123 on the clipboard.)

5. Explain why you should store your raw data in one location and work on a copy of that data instead.

Because some things can't be undone. If you sort only part of your data, for example, and don't realize it until later your entire dataset will be useless. Or if you find and replace the wrong information. Or you remove duplicates from only part of your data. Etc.

6. What's another best practice when doing a lot of complex work with a dataset that requires multiple steps and manipulations?

Save versions of the data as you go after each significant manipulation is completed. This way if you do mess up at some point along the way you can go back to one of those earlier versions rather than having to start over from scratch.

7. Why should you test your formulas before applying them to a large data set?

To make sure they're working properly, especially at the thresholds. So, for example, if you're using an IF function that returns one value when the value in Column A is over 25 and another value when it's under, you should test what happens when the value in Column A is 25. Is that the result you want? If not, you need to edit the formula. And it's easier to catch these things in test scenarios that are designed to test the edges than in a thousand rows of data.

8. Why can't you just accept the results Excel gives you? Why should you always "gut check" those results?

Because Excel just does what you tell it to do and if you tell it to do the wrong thing it's going to do it without question. So you should always be asking yourself, "does this result make sense"? And if it doesn't, you need to look at the numbers and your result to see if there's an error in your formula.

COPYING FORMULAS
QUIZ ANSWERS

1. What happens when you copy a formula from one cell to another?

All cell references in the formula will adjust based upon the number of rows and columns you moved the formula. So if a formula references Cell A1 and you move it over two columns, that reference to Cell A1 will become a reference to Cell C1. And if you move it down two rows, that reference to Cell A1 will become a reference to Cell A3.

2. If you write a formula and you want to fix the reference to a specific cell so that even if the formula is copied elsewhere it continues to reference that cell, how can you do this?

By using $ signs in front of both the column and row reference. So if you use $A$1 in a formula and copy that formula, the formula will continue to reference Cell A1 no matter where you copy it to.

3. What if you just want to lock the row reference but not the entire cell reference?

Then just put a $ sign in front of the row portion of the cell reference. So, for example, A$1.

4. What if you just want to lock the column reference but not the entire cell reference?

Then just put a $ sign in front of the column portion of the cell reference. So, for example, $A1.

5. If you just want to move a formula to a new location without it changing, what's the best way to do that?

Use Cut instead of Copy. That will move the formula without changing the cell references.

BASIC MATH FUNCTIONS
QUIZ ANSWERS

1. What is the function you can use to sum a range of values or a range of cells?
SUM

2. How would you write a function to sum the values in Column A?
=SUM(A:A)

3. How would you write a function to sum the values in Rows 1 through 3?
=SUM(1:3)

4. How would you write a function to sum the values in Columns A, C, and E?
=SUM(A:A,C:C,E:E)

5. How would you write a function to sum the values in Cells A1 through B6?
=SUM(A1:B6)

6. How would you write a function to subtract the total of all customer orders in Column C from the amount collected which is listed in Cell F1?

=F1-SUM(C:C)

7. What is the function you can use to multiply a range of values or a range of cells?

PRODUCT

8. If you want to multiply number of units in Cell A1 times unit price in Cell B1 times tax rate in Cell C1, how would you write that using a function?

=PRODUCT(A1,B1,C1) or =PRODUCT(A1:C1)

9. What is another way to do that that doesn't use a function?

=A1*B1*C1

10. What is the function you can use to multiply a range of values and then sum those results?

SUMPRODUCT

11. What are the inputs that go into that function?

You tell Excel the range of values that need to be multiplied times one another. So it's written as =SUMPRODUCT(array1, [array2], [array3],...) where each array is a range of cells to be multiplied one entry at a time times the corresponding entry in the other arrays.

12. If you have a table with number of units in Column A and unit price in Column B and you want to calculate the total earned (units times price and then summed across all rows), how would you write that using a single function?

=SUMPRODUCT(A:A,B:B)

13. What's another way to do that calculation?

You could also calculate the product for each row and then sum the total of those results.

14. When using SUMPRODUCT, what does the #VALUE! error message likely indicate?

That the arrays (or cell ranges) that you provided for the function are not the same size.

15. What does Excel do with text entries that are included in a SUMPRODUCT cell range?

Treats the text as a zero which means it will return a zero result for any line where one of the entries is text.

16. Can you use SUMPRODUCT for rows of data instead of columns?

Yes.

17. Is there a function for subtracting values from one another?

No.

18. Is there a function for dividing values by one another?

No.

19. Why?

Because with both subtraction and division the order of the inputs matters. With addition 2+3 and 3+2 give the same result, so you can have a function that adds a range of cells and it will work. But with subtraction 2-3 is not the same as 3-2 so you can't have a function that performs that task. Same with division.

20. If you have a series of a hundred numbers in Column B that you want to subtract from the value in Cell A1, how can you use a function to do that?

=A1-SUM(B:B)

AVERAGES, MEANS, AND MODES
QUIZ ANSWERS

1. What is the difference between an average, a mean, and a mode?

An average is an arithmetic mean of a series of numbers. It's calculated by adding those numbers together and then dividing by the count of the numbers you just added. So if I average 3, 4, and 5, the result is 4 because I add 3, 4, and 5 to get 12 and then divide by 3 to get 4.

The median value is the number in the middle of a range of values. Looking at the example above with 3, 4, and 5 the median value is also 4 because it's the middle value.

But let's change that up. Let's look at 3, 4, and 500 instead of 3, 4, and 5. The average of 3, 4, and 500 is 169 but the median is still 4 because the middle value in that range of numbers is 4. If you have data that is evenly distributed, the two numbers should be similar, but if there's a large skew in your data, then you'll want to look at both results because they could be quite different.

The mode returns the most frequently occurring or repetitive value in a range. It's basically telling you where there's a bump in your data. It's especially useful in situations where there is a heavy concentration of values and that concentration of values is not in the center of the range.

2. What's a good idea when dealing with a large range of data points that will help you figure out whether average, mean, or mode works best for your data?

Plot it. If you put your data points onto a scatter plot you will be able to see if there are any unusual concentrations in the data points or any sort of skew to your data that could impact the result of using average, mean, or mode.

3. If I want to calculate the average of values in Cells A1 through A5, how can I do that using a function?

=AVERAGE(A1:A5)

4. What happens if one of the cells in that range is blank?

Excel will ignore it. So it will sum the other four values and divide by four. It will not divide by five even though there were five cells in our specified range.

5. What can you do to make sure that Excel includes all cells within the specified range when using the AVERAGE function?

Put a zero in any blank cells so that they're included in the calculation.

6. What happens if one of the cells in that range contains text?

Excel will ignore it.

7. What can you do to make sure that Excel includes cells with text in them when calculating an average over a range of cells?

Use the AVERAGEA function instead. It will treat text entries and FALSE values as having a value of 0 and TRUE values as having a value of 1.

8. Can you take an average of the returns of a TRUE/FALSE series of responses to get the overall percent of responses that were true? How?

Yes. Using the AVERAGEA function.

9. If I have four cells with the values 2, 6, Other, and Now, what result will I get using AVERAGE? What result will I get using AVERAGEA?

AVERAGE will return a result of 4 which is 2+6 divided by 2. AVERAGEA will return a result of 2 which is 2+6 divided by 4.

10. How does AVERAGEA handle blank cells in a range?

It ignores them.

11. How would you write the function to calculate the median of a range of values from Cells C1 through C9?

=MEDIAN(C1:C9)

12. How does Excel calculate the median when there is an even number of values in the range?

It averages the middle two values.

13. Why can this be dangerous?

Because if you have data that's something like 1, 1, 100, 100, Excel will return a value of 50.5 even though that value is nowhere close to an actual value in the data.

14. Can you use median with TRUE/FALSE values?

Yes, if they're typed directly into the function. For example, =MEDIAN(TRUE, FALSE, FALSE)

15. What's a way to work around the need to type the TRUE and FALSE into the function itself?

Convert the TRUE/FALSE results into 1s and 0s and then you can reference the numbers using a cell range.

16. What function should you use to find the most common result when your data has a large bump that isn't near the midline?

MODE. Or, in recent versions of Excel, MODE.SNGL or MODE.MULT.

17. How would you write this function for a range of values in Cells B2 through B10?

=MODE(B2:B10) or MODE.SNGL(B2:B10)

18. What does MODE.MULT let you do?

Return more than one result when you have muti-modal data. (Meaning data that has more than one bump to it.)

19. What is special about the MODE.MULT function?

It's an array formula which means it returns results in more than one cell.

20. How do you use MODE.MULT?

Highlight the range of cells where you want Excel to return your results. If there are two bumps in the data, highlight two cells. If there are three, highlight three cells, etc. Only once you've done this should you type in your MODE.MULT function with the cell range you want to evaluate. And then, instead of hitting Enter, you hit Ctrl + Shift + Enter.

21. If you've properly used MODE.MULT, what will it look like in the formula bar when you click back into the cell for the function?

It will have curvy brackets at each end like this: {=MODE.MULT(A1:A10)}

22. If you have multi-modal data where two values occur with the same high frequency but you use the MODE.SNGL or MODE function instead of the MODE.MULT function, what will happen?

Excel will return the first value that occurs at that frequency. So if 5 and 25 both occur at an equally frequent high amount in the data, Excel will only return the 5 value.

23. What can you do if you want your MODE.MULT results to display in a row instead of in a column?

Write the formula as

=TRANSPOSE(MODE.MULT(A1:A10))

instead. The TRANSPOSE will flip the results from going down a column to going across a row.

24. What is one issue with MODE.MULT that you're still going to run into?

It's only going to return the most frequently occurring results. So if you have one value that occurs 10 times, another that occurs 10 times, and a third that occurs 9 times it will only return those first two values even though that third one may also be of interest to you.

25. How could you work around this issue?

Build a count table of your values that counts each value and its number of occurrences and then sort by count to see your top values that way.

MINIMUMS AND MAXIMUMS
QUIZ ANSWERS

1. If you want the minimum value within a range, what function can you use to get it?
    MIN or MINA

2. If you want the maximum value within a range, what function can you use to get it?
    MAX or MAXA

3. How would you write the function to calculate the minimum value in Column D?
    =MIN(D:D) or =MINA(D:D)

4. How would you write the function to calculate the maximum value in Row 3?
    =MAX(3:3) or =MAXA(3:3)

5. What value will Excel return if you ask for the minimum or maximum of a range of values that have no numbers in them?
    0

6. What will happen if you try to take the minimum or maximum of a range of values that has an error value in it such as #DIV/0!?

It will return the error value.

7. If you have a range of values that you want to take a minimum of but that range includes TRUE and FALSE entries that you want included in the calculation, what function should you use?

MINA

8. How do MINA and MAXA treat TRUE or FALSE values?

TRUE values are treated as a 1. FALSE values are treated as a 0.

9. How do MINA and MAXA treat text?

A text entry is treated as a zero.

10. What result will you get from =MINA(A1:A3) where A1 is the word Other, A2 is 2, and A3 is 3?

0

11. What result will you get from =MINA(A1:A3) where A1 is -2, A2 is 2, and A3 is 3?

-2

12. What result will you get from =MAXA(A1:A3) where A1 is -2, A2 is 2, and A3 is 3?

3

ROUNDING QUIZ ANSWERS

1. What functions can you use to round numbers?
ROUND, ROUNDUP, ROUNDDOWN

2. If you want to round a number to a specified number of digits and it can either be rounded up or down depending on which number it's closest to, which function should you use?
ROUND

3. If you want to round a number to a specified number of digits and you want to always round away from zero, which function should you use?
ROUNDUP

4. If you want to round a number to a specified number of digits and you want to always round towards zero, which function should you use?
ROUNDDOWN

5. What is the difference between using one of the rounding functions and just formatting a number to display a certain number of decimal places?

Formatting the number doesn't change the underlying value of that number. So 1.234 will still be 1.234 even if it looks like it's now just 1. Whereas applying ROUND to that number will change it into the number 1 and will remove the decimal places as if they never existed.

6. If you want to round the number 234.561 to the nearest whole number, how would you write that function?
=ROUND(234.561,0)

7. What if you wanted to round it to one decimal place?
=ROUND(234.561,1)

8. What if you wanted to round it to two decimal places?
=ROUND(234.561,2)

9. What if you wanted to round it to the nearest 100's (so 200)?
=ROUND(234.561,-2)

10. If I tell Excel to round a number to the nearest four decimal places, but there are only two decimal places in the number now, what will Excel do?
It'll leave the number as it is. =ROUND(2.34, 4) will return a value of 2.34.

11. How does Excel decide with the ROUND function whether to round up or to round down?
It looks at the digit one past where you told it to round and uses that to decide whether to round up or down. So if you have 1.2646 and tell Excel to round to two digits it will round down to 1.26 because of the 4 in the third position. It will not round up from the 6 to make the 4 a 5 and then round up from that. Digits from 0 through 4 round down. Digits from 5 through 9 round up.

12. If you use the **ROUNDUP** function to round to the nearest two decimal places for **1.239**, what will you get?

    1.24

13. If you use the **ROUNDDOWN** function to round to the nearest two decimal places for **1.239**, what will you get?

    1.23

14. If you use the **ROUNDUP** function to round to the nearest two decimal places for **1.231**, what will you get?

    1.24

15. If you use the **ROUNDDOWN** function to round to the nearest two decimal places for **1.231**, what will you get?

    1.23

16. If you use the **ROUNDUP** function to round to the nearest two decimal places for **-1.239**, what will you get?

    -1.24

17. If you use the **ROUNDDOWN** function to round to the nearest two decimal places for **-1.239**, what will you get?

    -1.23

18. If you use the **ROUNDUP** function to round to the nearest two decimal places for **-1.231**, what will you get?

    -1.24

19. If you use the **ROUNDDOWN** function to round to the nearest two decimal places for **-1.231**, what will you get?

    -1.23

20. What issue can you run into if you use ROUNDUP or ROUNDDOWN instead of ROUND?

It creates a small bias to always round in just one direction. If you use ROUND and the results are randomly distributed, then over time your rounding up and rounding down will balance out to a net result very close to zero. But if you always round up or always round down then over time as you do so more and more the total result will move more and more from the true result.

BASIC COUNT FUNCTIONS QUIZ
ANSWERS

1. What does the COUNT function allow you to do?

It allows you to count how many cells within the specified range have a number or date in them.

2. Does COUNT include cells with text in them?

No.

3. Does COUNT include cells with formulas in them that create a number or date?

Yes.

4. Does COUNT include cells with formulas in them that create a text entry?

No.

5. If a cell contains "1 unit" as its value, will COUNT count it?

No.

6. How would you use COUNT on a range of cells from B2 through D8?

=COUNT(B2:D8)

7. What function can you use if you also want to count cells that contain text in them?

COUNTA

8. What does this function allow you to do?

Count all cells in the range that are not empty.

9. What happens when you have a function in a cell, say =CONCATENATE(A1,B1,C1) but that cell is currently not displaying a value and you use each of the count functions?

COUNT will not count the cell. COUNTA will.

10. What should you always do when using any function?

Test to make sure that it's doing what you think it should be, including testing the COUNT functions to make sure that the cells you want counted are being counted.

11. What does COUNTBLANK do?

It counts the number of cells in the range that are empty. That means any cells that would return a value of "" but not cells with zero values or spaces in them.

12. If you have an issue with which cells are being counted by a specific count function, what should you do?

Look to the nature of the cells in question. Perhaps they look blank but have a space in them or they look blank but contain a function.

THE COUNTIFS, SUMIFS, AND AVERAGEIFS FUNCTIONS QUIZ ANSWERS

1. What is the difference between COUNTIFS, SUMIFS, and AVERAGEIFS?

COUNTIFS will count the number of entries that meet your specified criteria. SUMIFS will sum the values in a specified range of cells when your specified criteria are met. AVERAGEIFS will average the values in a specified range of cells when your specified criteria are met.

2. If you have access to both COUNTIF and COUNTIFS (or both SUMIF and SUMIFS, or both AVERAGEIF and AVERAGEIFS), which one should you use? Why?

Use the COUNTIFS, SUMIFS, or AVERAGEIFS versions because they can do everything their counterpart (COUNTIF, SUMIF, or AVERAGEIF) can do as well as handle multiple criteria. And since the order of the inputs is different, at least with SUMIFS and AVERAGEIFS, it's better to just always work with the more recent version of the function.

3. What is the difference between COUNTIF and COUNTIFS? What about SUMIF and SUMIFS? And AVERAGEIF and AVERAGEIFS?

COUNTIF can handle one criteria. COUNTIFS can handle multiple criteria. Same with the singular versions, SUMIF and AVERAGEIF, versus the plural versions, SUMIFS and AVERAGEIFS.

4. If you want to count how many times the values in Cells C10 through C25 are the same as the value in Cell A1, how would you write that function?

=COUNTIFS(C10:C25,A1)
or
=COUNTIF(C10:C25,A1)

5. What if you wanted to count how many times the cells in that range had text that included an e in it?

=COUNTIFS(C10:C25,"*e*")
or
=COUNTIF(C10:C25,"*e*")

6. Could you count how many cells from Cells C10 through C25 have the same values as Cell A1 AND how many have an e in them? If so, how would you write that and what issue would you potentially run into?

You could, but you'd have to use two COUNTIFS functions to do it and if it turned out the value in Cell A1 had an e in it, you could end up double-counting cells because you had to use two COUNTIFS functions.

=COUNTIFS(C10:C23,A1)+COUNTIFS(C10:C23,"*e*")
or
=COUNTIF(C10:C23,A1)+ COUNTIF(C10:C23,"*e*")

7. If you want to count how many times the values in Cells C10 through C25 are greater than the value in Cell A1, how would you write that?

=COUNTIFS(C10:C25,">"&A1)
or
=COUNTIF(C10:C25,">"&A1)

8. If you want to count how many customers are from Alaska and have bought Widgets when your customer location is stored in Column C and your product is stored in Column E, how would you write that?

=COUNTIFS(C:C,"Alaska",E:E,"Widgets")

9. If you want to count how many customers have bought more than 10 of your product and are from Hawaii when customer location is stored in Column C and number of units is in Column D, how would you write that?

=COUNTIFS(C:C,"Hawaii",D:D,">10")

10. If you want to count how many times Student A scored over 90 and Student B scored over 90 when their test scores are recorded in Rows 2 and 3, how would you do that?

=COUNTIFS(2:2,">90",3:3,">90")

11. What do you need to watch out for when using COUNTIFS, SUMIFS, and AVERAGEIFS?

That your cell ranges for each of your criteria are properly lined up. If your data is stored across columns then you want to make sure your data starts with the same row number for all criteria, for example, so that Excel is looking at the values for the criteria in those columns across the same row. (Assuming that's how your data is set up. As long as the cell ranges are the same size, Excel can work with it, but remember, garbage in, garbage out.)

12. If you want to total the value of all customer orders, which is listed in Column H, for all customers from Maine, which is listed in Column C, and who bought Widgets, which is listed in Column E, how would you do that?

=SUMIFS(H:H,C:C,"Maine",E:E,"Widgets")

13. Can you total the value of all customer orders over $100 using SUMIF or SUMIFS? How would you write that assuming customer order value is listed in Column H?

Yes.

=SUMIF(H:H,">100")

or

=SUMIFS(H:H,H:H,">100")

14. What do the asterisk (*), the question mark (?), and the tilde (~) represent when you're writing a count, sum, or average criteria?

The asterisk is a wildcard that represents any number of characters. The question mark is a wildcard that represents one single character. The tilde is a symbol you can use before an asterisk or question mark to indicate that that's actually what you wanted to search for rather than it being a wild card.

15. Can you calculate the average customer order for a customer in Colorado who made a purchase in June, assuming that customer order is stored in Column H, customer location is in Column C, and purchase month is in Column B? How would you write that?

Yes.

=AVERAGEIFS(H:H,C:C,"Colorado",B:B,"June")

16. If there are no customer transactions that meet that criteria what result is Excel going to return?
#DIV/0!

17. With COUNTIFS, SUMIFS, and AVERAGEIFS, if you have three criteria you specify and two of the three are met, what will happen with that entry?
It will not be included in the calculation. All of the criteria you specify must be met for Excel to count the entry or include its value in the sum or average calculation.

18. Why is this important?
Because if you write one of your criteria wrong, your function is not going to work properly. Remember to test, test, test your function, especially along the borders. So if your criteria is all entries over 100, test 101 and 100 to see what result you get.

BASIC TEXT FUNCTIONS
QUIZ ANSWERS

1. If you want to convert a text string into uppercase letters, which function should you use?
UPPER

2. What if you want to convert a text string into lowercase letters?
LOWER

3. What if you want the initial letter of each word to be capitalized, but the rest to be in lowercase?
PROPER

4. Let's say that you have a text string in Cell C10 and another in Cell C11 and that you want to combine those entries with a space between them and convert them into uppercase letters. How could you do that?
Once solution would be:
=UPPER(CONCATENATE(C10," ",C11))

5. What does CONCATENATE do?
Allows you to join several "text" strings into one. Text strings can be cell references or actual text that you input,

including spaces and symbols.

6. What is the difference between proper case and title case?

Proper case capitalizes the first letter of every single word. Title case capitalizes the first letter of significant words but does not capitalize smaller filler words like of, or, the, and, etc.

7. What does the LEFT function do?

It returns the first x number of characters from the left-hand side of a text string.

8. If you want to return the first five characters of the text in Cell A1, how would you do that?

=LEFT(A1,5)

9. Does this function work with numbers as well?

Yes.

10. What happens if the number of characters you specify is greater than the number of characters in the string you reference?

Excel returns the entire result.

11. What happens if you don't specify a number of characters to return?

Excel will default to a value of 1 and just return the first character.

12. For languages that don't work with characters, like Chinese, Japanese, and Korean, which function will do the same for those languages?

LEFTB

13. If you want to return the last two characters of a text string, how can you do that?

Using the RIGHT function.

14. What does the MID function do?

It returns the specified number of characters from a text string given a starting position. So if you tell it to go three characters in and then return the next three characters, it can do that.

15. What happens if the start point you provide for the MID function is greater than the number of characters in the string?

Excel returns an empty result.

16. What happens if you use MID and ask Excel to return more characters than there are in the text string?

It will return what there is.

17. What other function could you use to get the same result as =MID(A1,1,2)?

=LEFT(A1,2)

18. If you want to take a text string and remove all spaces from it except for one space between each word, which function can you use to do that?

TRIM

19. If you had a list of entries with first name, middle name, and last name in separate columns, Columns A, B, and C, and you wanted to combine those entries for each row into one entry with only one space between each word, and you knew that not every entry had a middle name, how could you use two functions to do that in one cell? Write the function for Row 1.

=TRIM(CONCATENATE(A1," ",B1," ",C1))

20. What do you need to be careful of when using any

of the above functions? What can you do when you're done with your manipulation to address this?

Your text entry is still a formula, meaning that if you change the values in the input cells (by, for example, deleting them) you will change the result of your formula. This is why it's a good idea once you're done with manipulating your text strings to copy and paste special-values to lock in the result as a text entry and remove the formulas. (But only do that when you're done and don't expect the inputs to change further.)

21. What type of inputs will CONCATENATE accept? And how do they need to be written?

Cell references, numbers, or text. Cell references can be written as they are (B1). Numbers can be written as they are or in quotes (32 or "32"). Text must be written in quotes ("text").

22. If you want there to be a space or a comma in your final CONCATENATE result, how do you do that?

Make it a text element in your function. So for that text element start with a quote mark and then add your space and/or comma and then close with a quote mark. Each text element in a CONCATENATE function is separated by a comma. For example, to create Jones, Albert where Jones was in Cell B1 and Albert was in Cell A1, you could write =CONCATENATE(B1,", ",A1) where the ", " is the second text element in the formula.

23. With CONCATENATE if you get a NAME#? error, what has generally gone wrong?

You likely failed to put quotation marks around a text element.

24. What function is Excel replacing CONCATENATE with?

CONCAT. It's in versions of Excel from 2016 onward.

THE TEXT FUNCTION
QUIZ ANSWERS

1. What does Excel say that the TEXT function can do?

Convert a value to text in a specific number format.

2. What else can the TEXT function actually do?

Extract information from a date. You can use TEXT to return the day of the week, month of the year, or a time component from a date. And with day of the week or month of the year that can be the written form of the date, so December or Dec, for example.

3. If you have a date in Cell A1 and want to pull the full name of the day of the week, how would you do that using the TEXT function?

=TEXT(A1,"dddd")

4. What about the month of the year?

=TEXT(A1,"mmmm")

5. If you use TEXT to create number formats, for example =TEXT(A1,"$0.00"), what issue can you run into?

Sometimes Excel will create numbers you never wanted. For example, if you use the wrong characters, you can end up with a whole number followed by a decimal with no numbers after the decimal (5.). Or you can end up with a whole number followed by a decimal followed by a space followed by another number (5. 1). Try, for example, =TEXT(5,"$?.??) to see what I mean.

6. What is the other thing to be aware of when using the TEXT function with a number?

It converts your entry into text, so it's no longer treated as a number by Excel. This means you can't do calculations on it anymore.

7. What's one quick way to see valid number formats you can use with the TEXT function?

Right-click on a cell, choose Format Cells, go to the Number tab, and choose Custom. You'll see a number of options there for how to format numbers that you can translate to the TEXT function. Excel won't accept all of them for the TEXT function, but it is a good start.

8. If you wanted to return the number value in Cell A1 as "50% Win Rate", how could you do that using TEXT?

=TEXT(A1,"00.00%")&" Win Rate" (Note that *50 Useful Functions* has an error in the text for this one. A1 would need to be .5 for this to return a value of 50% not 50 like the book says.)

THE TODAY AND NOW
FUNCTIONS QUIZ ANSWERS

1. What does the TODAY function do?

Returns the current date formatted as a date.

2. How do you write it?

=TODAY()

3. Why would you use it?

Because it helps as part of a calculation that's looking at how many days from today something needs to happen or did happen. For example, days past due on payment.

4. If you wanted to calculate how many days it's been since someone purchased your product, which is the better option: have a cell that uses =TODAY() and then another cell that calculates days since purchase or just have a cell that calculates days since purchase and incorporates TODAY() into the formula? Why?

It's better to have the TODAY() function in its own cell so that all assumptions are visible. This way you can confirm that the worksheet updated. when you opened it.

Also, there will be times when someone isn't expecting the worksheet to have updated so having that visible makes it obvious what's happened.

5. What does the NOW function do?

Returns the current date *and time* formatted as a date and time.

6. What's the difference between using TODAY and NOW?

TODAY will return today's date with a time of midnight. NOW will return today's date with the current time.

7. Why does this matter?

Because if you intend to use formulas to calculate differences between two times and it doesn't matter to you that that calculation be accurate down to the minute, you should be using TODAY instead of NOW.

8. What do you need to be aware of when using both TODAY and NOW?

That they update whenever you open your worksheet, when you press F9, and when you do any other calculation in your worksheet. So if you need to capture the time right now and then preserve that value, you'll need to take steps to replace that value with a fixed value instead of a function.

9. How does Excel treat dates for the purpose of addition and subtraction?

It converts the hours for a day into a decimal. So 12 hours is equivalent to .5 since it's half a day. The number 5 would represent 5 whole days.

10. So if you wanted to calculate the date five and a half days from today's date, what could you use?

=TODAY()+5.5

11. What if you wanted to calculate the date and time exactly five and a half days from this moment?
=NOW()+5.5

12. Is it possible that those two formulas could return different dates?
Yes.

THE IF FUNCTION
QUIZ ANSWERS

1. What does an IF function do?

It allows you to return different results depending on whether the criteria you specify are met or not.

2. Translate the IF function =IF(A2>25,0,A2*0.05) into a written description.

IF Cell A2 has a value greater than 25 then return a value of zero. Otherwise, return a value equal to the value in Cell A2 times .05.

3. What is another way to think about the components of an IF function?

IF(If, Then, Else) or IF A, THEN B, ELSE C or IF A, THEN B, OTHERWISE C.

4. What does it mean that you can nest IF functions?

It means that you can start with one IF function and then replace either the THEN component or the ELSE component with another IF function so that you get IF A, THEN B, ELSE, IF C, THEN D, OTHERWISE E, for example.

5. If you're going to nest IF functions, which is it better to replace, the Then portion or the Else portion? Why?

The Else portion. Because then that keeps all of the parts of each individual IF function together as opposed to splitting them up across the function.

6. Translate the IF function =IF(A9>$A$5,$B$5,IF (A9>$A$4,$B$4,0)) into a written description.

If the value in Cell A9 is greater than the value in Cell A5, then return the value in Cell B5. Otherwise, if the value in Cell A9 is greater than the value in Cell A4, return the value in Cell B4. Otherwise return a value of zero.

7. If you were to copy the above formula into a new cell, how would it change?

The only thing that would change is the cell reference to cell A9, the rest of the function uses $ signs to refer to specified cells. It's using a table to generate the results of the IF function.

8. If you have a long and complex nested IF function that you can't get to work, what are some ways you can troubleshoot the IF function to figure out what's wrong?

Arrow through the function to make sure that you have the correct number of opening and closing parens. For each IF in the function there should be one opening paren immediately after the IF and a corresponding closing paren somewhere in the function.

Replace all but one of the IF functions with a placeholder result to create a simple IF function and evaluate whether it's doing what it should. So, for example,

=IF(A9>$A$5,$B$5,IF(A9>$A$4,$B$4,0))

would become

=IF(A9>$A$5,$B$5,"ELSE")

where the second IF function has temporarily been replaced with a result of ELSE.

9. What is the most likely issue if Excel tells you you've entered too many arguments with an IF function?

You probably have a misplaced paren somewhere. (Older versions of Excel did limit the number of IF functions you could nest, but in current versions you're unlikely to have too many IF functions nested.)

10. What should you always do with an IF function that you create? (Or any function really?)

Test it to make sure it's doing what it should be. Pay particular attention to threshold results where the result should transition from one result to another. For example, did you mean greater than or did you mean greater than or equal to and how did you actually write it?

11. If you write an IF function that's referencing a table of fixed values (like a discount table) what should you always be sure to do?

Use $ signs when writing the references to those cells so that you can easily copy your IF function while keeping the table references fixed.

VLOOKUP QUIZ ANSWERS

1. What does VLOOKUP do?

Looks for a value in the leftmost column of a cell range and then returns a value in the same row for a column you specify.

2. What must you do if you're using VLOOKUP on a table?

Sort your data using the values in that first column.

3. What's the best use for VLOOKUP?

Finding values in a reference table that's built to be used with the function.

4. Do the values in a reference table need to be an exact match for the value you're looking for for VLOOKUP to work?

No.

5. What is the minimum number of columns your data needs for VLOOKUP to work?

One. You can use VLOOKUP to look up the closest result to your lookup value.

6. Can the column that has the values you're looking up be located anywhere in your data?

No. It must be the left-most column in the range you specify. It doesn't have to be the left-most column in your data but it must be the left-most column in the range and it must be to the left of the column with the values you want to return.

7. How do you tell Excel whether to look for an exact match or an approximate match?

With the fourth element of your function. If you say TRUE or 1, it will look for an approximate match. If you say FALSE or 0, it will look for an exact match only.

8. What is the difference between an exact match and an approximate match?

An exact match will only return a result when what you're looking for is an exact match to an entry in the data table. An approximate match will return a result that's closest to the value you're looking for.

9. What is =VLOOKUP(25,A1:E10,3,FALSE) saying to do?

Lookup the value of 25 in Column A of a cell range that starts in Cell A1 and ends in Cell E10. If there is a value of 25 in the that column then return the value in the row that contains the value of 25 from Column C.

10. What is =VLOOKUP(25,A1:E10,2,TRUE) saying to do?

Lookup the value of 25 in Column A of a cell range that starts in Cell A1 and ends in Cell E10. Find the row in Column A of the table that is either equal to 25 or directly before the first row that has a value of more than 25 and return the value in Column B of that row.

11. What do you need to be careful of when using VLOOKUP with apparent numbers or dates?

If the numbers or dates are stored as text, they may produce unexpected results.

12. What should you always do when using any function in Excel?

Test to make sure that the result you get makes sense.

THE AND & OR FUNCTIONS
QUIZ ANSWERS

1. What does the AND function do?

Checks to see if all arguments are true or not. If so, it returns TRUE. If not, it returns FALSE.

2. What does the OR function do?

Checks to see if any of the arguments listed are true. If so, it returns TRUE. If not, it returns FALSE.

3. What is =AND(A1>5,A2>4) asking?

Is it true that the value in A1 is greater than five and that the value in A2 is greater than 4?

4. What is =OR(A1>5,A2>4) asking?

Is either the value in A1 greater than five or the value in A2 greater than 4?

5. What is =AND(A1>B1,A2>B2) asking?

Is the value in A1 greater than the value in B1 and is the value in A2 greater than B2.

6. What is =IF(AND(A1="Jones",B1="Whatsit"), C1,D1) doing?

It's saying that if the value in Cell A1 is Jones and the value in B1 is Whatsit then return the value in C1, otherwise return the value in D1.

7. What is =IF(OR(A1="Canton",B1="Toledo"), G1,G1*2) doing?

It's saying that if the value in Cell A1 is either Canton or Toledo then return the value in G1. If it isn't, then return a value of G1 times two.

THE TRUE, FALSE AND NA
FUNCTIONS QUIZ ANSWERS

1. What do the TRUE and FALSE functions do?

They return a value of TRUE or FALSE.

2. When might you use them?

When you're using functions that return different results for a TRUE or FALSE result. Sometimes simply typing TRUE or FALSE doesn't create the same result as using TRUE() and FALSE() the functions. For example, say you wanted to use AVERAGEA on the results of an IF function. You could have the IF function return a result of TRUE or FALSE and then apply AVERAGEA to those results.

3. What does the NA function do?

Returns the error value #N/A.

4. When might you use the NA function?

To mark empty cells when using a formula. If you return an empty space instead of an N/A result some functions won't work properly. This can be especially useful when having to graph results since Excel will skip N/A values whereas it will not skip empty results.

5. What do you need to remember when using the TRUE, FALSE, or NA functions?

That you always need to include the parens after the function name. So write TRUE() not TRUE.

RANDOM NUMBERS
QUIZ ANSWERS

1. What function will return a random number greater than or equal to 0 and less than 1 evenly distributed?
 RAND

2. What function will return a random whole number between two values you specify?
 RANDBETWEEN

3. If I want to return any possible value, including a decimal value between 0 and 100, how can I do that?
 =100*RAND()

4. If I want to return any whole number between 0 and 100, how can I do that?
 =RANDBETWEEN(0,100) or =INT(RAND()*100)

5. What do you need to be careful of when using either function?
 It will generate a new random value every time you recalculate your worksheet with F9, every time you do

another calculation in your worksheet, and every time you open the worksheet and you won't be able to go back to the previously-generated value.

6. How can you work around this if you need to capture that value?

Generate your random value and then use copy and paste special-values to convert the entry to a value instead of keep it as a function.

RANKING QUIZ ANSWERS

1. What function or functions can you use if you want to know the rank of a specific value within a range of possible values? In other words, is this the 5th largest number, the 10th, the 20th, etc. compared to other numbers in the range?

RANK, RANK.EQ, or RANK.AVG

2. If you want to know the rank of a value in Cell A1 from within the range of Cells A1 through A15, how can you write that function using ascending values?

=RANK(A1,A1:A15,1)
or
=RANK.EQ(A1,A1:A15,1)
or
=RANK.AVG(A1,A1:A15,1)

3. What about using descending values?

=RANK(A1,A1:A15,0)
or

=RANK(A1,A1:A15)
or
=RANK.EQ(A1,A1:A15)
or
=RANK.AVG(A1,A1:A15)

4. To use the functions does your data have to be sorted?

No.

5. What happens if you use RANK on a data set where there are multiples of a value?

All instances of that value are assigned the same rank and then Excel skips however many ranks it needs to to account for that. So you can end up with ranks of 1, 2, 2, 2, and 5 for a dataset that has the values 2, 3, 3, 3, and 4.

6. How do RANK.EQ and RANK.AVG differ?

In how they treat instances where there is more than one of a result. For RANK.EQ it works like RANK and all ties are assigned the highest possible rank for that value and then Excel skips however many ranks it needs to. For RANK.AVG Excel takes the possible ranks for those tied values and returns an average for the ranks. (See the guide for a detailed discussion of how this works.)

THE SMALL AND LARGE FUNCTIONS QUIZ ANSWERS

1. What does the SMALL function do?

Returns the k-th smallest value in a data set where you specify the value of k.

2. What does the LARGE function do?

Returns the k-th largest value in a data set where you specify the value of k.

3. Can you technically use SMALL to return the largest value in a range and LARGE to return the smallest value in a range?

Yes. As long as you know the size of your range and use a k that's equal to that number.

4. What does the ROWS function do?

It counts the number of rows in your selection.

THE IFNA AND IFERROR QUIZ ANSWERS

1. What function can you use to suppress an #N/A! result in a formula?

The IFNA function.

2. Apply that function to the following formula: =VLOOKUP(D:D,'Advertising Spend By Series'!E:F, 2,FALSE) so that a value of 0 is returned instead of the #N/A! error message.

=IFNA(VLOOKUP(D:D,'Advertising Spend By Series'!E:F,2,FALSE),0)

3. Now apply the function to the following formula: =VLOOKUP(D:D,'Advertising Spend By Series'!E:F, 2,FALSE)so that a value of "No Match" is returned instead of the #N/A! error message.

=IFNA(VLOOKUP(D:D,'Advertising Spend By Series'!E:F,2,FALSE),"No Match")

4. And also apply the function to the following formula: =VLOOKUP(D:D,'Advertising Spend By

Series'!E:F,2,FALSE) so that a blank value is returned instead of the #N/A! error message.

=IFNA(VLOOKUP(D:D,'Advertising Spend By Series'!E:F,2,FALSE),"")

5. What function can you use to suppress all error messages instead of just #N/A!?

The IFERROR function.

6. Apply that function to a situation where you are dividing the value in Cell A1 by the value in Cell B1 and you want to return a blank result instead of an error message.

=IFERROR(A1/B1,"")

7. Now apply that function to a situation where you are dividing the value in Cell A1 by the value in Cell B1 and you want to return a value of "Error" instead of a specific error message.

=IFERROR(A1/B1,"Error")

8. What is the danger in using IFNA or IFERROR?

They may suppress a legitimate error message that you need to see. A #N/A! error can indicate that you have, for example, a formatting or spelling error in a list of values. And a #DIV/0! error can indicate you're missing a value you thought you had or that you're using the wrong cell in your equation.

9. What is one way of addressing this issue?

Have the formula return a text value instead of a value of zero or a blank value. This will indicate that an error message was generated by the calculation so that you can properly review it without interfering with any calculations on those cells.

THE NOT FUNCTION QUIZ ANSWERS

1. What functions is the NOT function related to?
The AND and OR functions.

2. Why do I encourage you to find a way to use a function other than the NOT function to build a formula?
Because using a negative to build a formula is counter to how most people think.

3. What result will you get if you use =NOT(FALSE)?
TRUE

4. What result will you get if you use =NOT(TRUE)?
FALSE

5. How could you use the NOT function?
To evaluate whether a criteria was met in a more complex formula.

6. Take the formula =NOT(B5<12). What value will it return if the value in Cell B5 is 2? What about if it's 14?
FALSE. TRUE.

7. How could you evaluate that condition (whether B5 is less than 12 or equal to or greater than 12) with an IF function and get the same result as using the NOT function above?

=IF(B5>12,TRUE) or =IF(B5>12,TRUE,FALSE)

THE HLOOKUP FUNCTION QUIZ ANSWERS

1. What function is the HLOOKUP function related to?

The VLOOKUP function.

2. What does HLOOKUP do?

It scans across a row of data to match a value you specify and then pulls a result from another row in the same column where that match was made. For example, you could scan for a month in a table with month values across the top and then pull the specific result for a vendor if vendor results were listed in rows below each month.

3. What will this formula do:
=HLOOKUP("April",B1:M12,4,FALSE)

It will look for a cell with the value "April" in row one of the data set contained in Cells B1 through M12 and then will go to the fourth row of that column and pull the value in the corresponding cell. In this case, a value will only be returned if there is an exact match to "April".

4. What can you look up using HLOOKUP?

A numeric value, a text string, or a cell reference.

5. If you look up a text string, what do you need to be sure to do?

Put quotation marks around the text string you want to look up.

6. What are wildcards and how can you use them when looking up text?

A wildcard, like * or ?, allows you to look up text without being exact about what text you're looking up. For example, "*April" would look up any text string that has April at the very end no matter how long the text string. So it would include "I like the month of April" as a valid match. On the other hand, "?April" will look for any text string that has one character before April. So "1April" would be a valid match but "20th April" would not.

7. In the table you're going to search using HLOOKUP, where do the values you're searching for need to be?

The first row of the range specified in the function.

8. In the table you're going to search using HLOOKUP, where do the values you want to return need to be?

In the lookup row or in the rows below the lookup row.

9. What is the difference between using FALSE and TRUE as the final input to the HLOOKUP function?

Using FALSE means that only an exact match will return a value. Using TRUE will return an approximate value.

10. What is the risk to using TRUE as the third input to the HLOOKUP function?

If your data isn't sorted in ascending order before you use the function, the value returned may not be the closest value.

11. Can you sort the values in a row in ascending order?

Yes. It's an option under the Sort function in Excel. Choose the Sort Left to Right option.

12. When you tell Excel which row to pull your result from using HLOOKUP, what number do you need to provide? Is it the Row number in the worksheet or something else?

No, it is not the row number in the worksheet. It's the row within the table specified in the HLOOKUP function.

13. If you provide a row value of 1 in the HLOOKUP function what will that return?

Either the value you were looking if you were looking for an exact match (FALSE) or the closest value if you were looking for an approximate value (TRUE).

14. If you ask HLOOKUP to find an exact match and there isn't one, what value will Excel return?

#N/A!

15. What could potentially result in an incorrect error message when using HLOOKUP?

A spelling error in the formula, extra spaces in the entries that are being looked at, an incorrect table range, incorrect row references, or a lookup value outside the range in the table.

THE TRANSPOSE FUNCTION QUIZ
ANSWERS

1. What does the TRANSPOSE function do?

It converts a vertical range of cells to a horizontal range or vice versa. In other words, it take a range of values in a row and puts them in a column or takes a range of values in a column and puts them in a row instead.

2. Does TRANSPOSE work on a table of values that covers multiple rows and/or columns?

Yes.

3. What do you have to do special because TRANSPOSE is an array formula?

Two things. You must first select the range of cells where you want your result to go before you start typing your formula in the first cell of the range. And you must also use Ctrl+Shift+Enter when you finish entering the formula (rather than just Enter) for it to work.

4. If you want to take the values in Cells C1 through C5 and place them in Cells E8 through I8, how would you do that?

Highlight Cells E8 through I8. Type in the formula

=TRANSPOSE(C1:C5) in Cell E8 (while keeping the other cells highlighted). Finish with Ctrl+Shift+Enter.

5. If all you want to do is change the orientation of your data, what is a better option?

Use Copy and Paste-Transpose instead.

6. What benefit does the TRANSPOSE function give over doing that?

When you use the TRANSPOSE function the values in your cells are still linked to their original source, so a change in the value in the original location will change the transposed value as well. When you use Copy and Paste-Transpose those pasted values are now separate from the original source values..

THE INDEX FUNCTION QUIZ
ANSWERS

1. What are the two tasks that the INDEX function can perform?

It can either return a single value in a specified position in a table or it can return a range of values in a specified location.

2. What is the following formula supposed to do: =INDEX(A2:E7,3,4)

Return the value in the third row of the fourth column of the data composed of Cells A2 through E7.

3. Does the INDEX function require you to include a header row or row labels in the specified cell range?

No. It's just returning a value in a specific location in a defined range.

4. How do you determine the row number value to use in the INDEX function?

It should be the number that corresponds to the order of the row within the defined range. It is not the actual row number in the Excel worksheet.

5. How do you determine the column number value to use in the INDEX function?

It should be the number that corresponds to the order of the column within the defined range. It is not the actual column number in the Excel worksheet.

6. Can you use the INDEX function with more than one table of data? How?

Yes. There is an optional fourth variable that can be included in the INDEX function that specifies which data table to pull the value from. In order to use it you have to provide multiple table ranges in the first input.

7. What happens if you use the fourth variable in the INDEX function without providing multiple table range values in the first variable?

You will get a #REF! error message.

8. If you want to use the INDEX function to pull an entire column or row of data, what do you need to do?

Use the function as an array formula. This means you highlight the cells where you want that data to go first, enter the formula in the first cell of that highlighted range, and then use Ctrl+Shift+Enter instead of Enter when you're done. To pull an entire column leave the row variable blank or set it to zero. To pull an entire row leave the column variable blank or set it to zero. For example, =INDEX(A2:E7,2,) and =INDEX(A2:E7,,3), will pull the entire second row and entire third column, respectively.

9. Can you easily copy and paste an array formula?

No.

10. Once you've extracted values from a table using the INDEX function are the results fixed values?

No. This is still a formula, so it's still pulling those values from the source table and any changes to the source table will change the values you pulled. The only way to fix the values is to then take the results and Copy and Paste Special-Values to remove the formula but keep the values.

THE MATCH FUNCTION QUIZ
ANSWERS

1. What does the MATCH function do?

It returns the relative position of an item in a specified range of cells. It can also return the relative position of the closest value if there is no exact match in the range of cells as long as the values in the cells are properly sorted.

2. If the MATCH function returns a value of 2 for the following formula, what does that mean:
=MATCH($A12,$A$2:$A$7,0)

That an exact match to the value in Cell A12 is in the second row of the data in the range from Cell A2 through Cell A7. The first value is the value you're looking for, the second is the range of cells where that value may be, and the third value says that it should be an exact match.

3. What is the value in using the MATCH function?

It can be combined with other functions, like the INDEX function to facilitate looking up values in data tables.

4. What kinds of values can MATCH look for?

Numeric, text values, or logical values.

5. What are the three match types that you can use with MATCH?

You can look for an exact match, the smallest value that is greater than or equal to the specified value, or the largest value that is less than or equal to the specified value.

6. If you're not looking for an exact match what do you need to do first? And how will your choice of match type impact this?

You need to sort your data. If you're looking for the smallest value that is greater than the specified value sort in descending order. If you're looking for the largest value that is less than the specified value sort in ascending order.

7. What is the default match type used by MATCH? Why is this a problem?

If you don't specify a match type (-1,0,1) then Excel will assume you wanted to use the 1 match type and will look for the largest value that is less than or equal to the specified value. This is a problem if you haven't sorted your data to accommodate that type of match.

8. Is the value returned by MATCH the row number or the column number in the worksheet or something else?

It is not the row or column number in the worksheet. It is the relative row number or relative column number within the specified cell range.

TEXT FUNCTIONS QUIZ ANSWERS

1. What does the LEN function do?

It returns the number of characters in a text string.

2. What does the SEARCH function do?

It returns the number of the character at which a specific character or text string can first be found, reading from left to right.

3. What does the FIND function do?

It returns the starting position of one text string within another text string.

4. So what is the difference between SEARCH and FIND?

FIND is case-sensitive, so will treat "This" and "this" differently. It also does not allow the use of wildcards where SEARCH does allow them.

5. If you're working in a language such as Japanese, Chinese, or Korean that uses bytes instead of characters what functions should you use instead of LEN, SEARCH, and FIND?

LENB, SEARCHB, and FINDB.

6. What does the EXACT function do?

It returns a value of TRUE or FALSE based upon whether two text strings are exactly the same or not.

7. Is EXACT case-sensitive?

Yes. It will return a value of FALSE if used on "This" and "this", for example.

8. What result would LEN return for =LEN("This one")? Why?

8. Because it includes the space between "this" and "one" in the count of length.

9. Can you use LEN with a cell reference, so for example, =LEN(D10)?

Yes.

10. How does LEN handle a formula in a cell?

It returns a count of the length of the result of the formula. So if the formula returned a value of 8, then LEN would return a value of 1 in reference to that cell.

11. What is the following formula doing: =LEFT(A1,LEN(A1)-LEN(" units"))?

It's taking the left n-most characters from Cell A1 where n is equal to the total number of characters in Cell A1 minus the number of characters in " units". This is a way to extract the numeric value from an entry such as 12,000 units or 500 units where the number of characters in the numeric portion of the value is an unknown.

12. How could you accomplish the same task using the SEARCH function? Explain why this works.

=LEFT(A1,SEARCH(" units",A1)-1)

In this formula SEARCH returns the point at which

" units" can be found in the text contained in Cell A1. But we don't want that value because that would include the space in the result. So we take that value and subtract one from it to get just the number of units.

13. Do you have to start at the beginning of a text string if using the SEARCH or FIND functions?

No. You can use the optional third input to specify where in the text string to start the search.

14. If you do use the third input in the SEARCH or FIND function, what do you need to keep in mind about the value that's returned?

That even though you started at a point somewhere within the text string the numeric value returned is still going to be based upon the entire length of the text string. So if you used a 5 for that last value and the result was 7 that means it was only two characters past the fifth character in the string and seven from the beginning of the text string.

15. What will your result be if the value you search for using SEARCH or FIND isn't in that text string?

#VALUE!

16. What will your result be if the start position you provide is a negative number or a larger number than the length of the text string in SEARCH or FIND?

#VALUE!

17. What values will =SEARCH("coz*","teacozy") and =FIND("coz*","teacozy") return? Why?

SEARCH will return a value of 4. FIND will return a value of #VALUE!. That's because FIND does not work with wildcard characters like the * or the ?.

18. What values will =SEARCH("t","Teapot") and =FIND("t","Teapot") return? Why?

SEARCH will return a value of 1. FIND will return a value of 6. This is because FIND is case-sensitive, but SEARCH is not.

19. Does EXACT look for differences in formatting between two entries?

No.

20. If you wanted to compare the values in Cells A1 and D2, how would you write that using the EXACT function? What value would you expect if the two values were equal? What would you expect if they were not?

=EXACT(A1,D2)
TRUE. FALSE.

21. If you use EXACT with two cells that use different formulas but return the same numeric value, what will the result be?

TRUE. The EXACT function looks at the values returned by the two formulas and compares them to see if they're equal.

THE CONVERT FUNCTION QUIZ
ANSWERS

1. What does the CONVERT function do?

It converts a number from one measurement system to another.

2. Name three types of conversions CONVERT can do:

Answers can include: Temperatures, distances, weights, units of time, units of energy, fluid measurements, speeds, etc.

3. What happens if you use units from two different categories in the same CONVERT function?

You'll receive an #N/A! error result.

4. Are the units used in the CONVERT function case-sensitive?

Yes. For example, "day" is a valid unit entry, but "Day" is not.

5. Write the formula for converting 57 degrees Fahrenheit to Celsius:

=CONVERT(57,"F","C")

6. Write the formula for determining how many days there are in five years using the CONVERT function:

=CONVERT(5,"yr","day")

7. Give a likely explanation for why the value returned in the last example is a decimal:

Because of leap years. There is one leap year every fourth year, so the calculation involves one-quarter of a day extra per year to account for that.

8. Write the formula for converting 60 miles to kilometers:

=CONVERT(60,"mi","km")

NUMERIC FUNCTIONS QUIZ
ANSWERS

1. What function would you use to take the absolute value of a number?

ABS

2. Write the function for the absolute value of -3:

=ABS(-3)

3. What does the MOD function do?

It takes one number divided by another and returns just the remainder.

4. What does the QUOTIENT function do?

It takes one number divided by another and returns just the integer portion of the resulting value.

5. Can you use the MOD and QUOTIENT functions to take a decimal number, such as 12.345 and separate the integer portion from the decimal portion? If so, how?

Yes. Assume the number is in Cell D3, you could use =MOD(D3,1) to extract the decimal portion and =QUOTIENT(D3,1) to extract the integer portion. This works because the division you're doing first keeps the number you started with.

6. What is another function that allows you to extract just the integer portion of a number?

The TRUNC function.

7. Apply this function to 12.345 to get 12:

=TRUNC(12.345,0) or =TRUNC(12.345)

8. What is the difference between truncating a number and rounding a number?

Truncating a number simply cuts the number off at that specific point. Rounding a number will take it to the next closest value based on rounding rules. So, for example, take the number 12.75 truncated or rounded. Truncating it will return a value of 12. Rounding it will return a value of 13.

9. How would you truncate 12,543 to the nearest 1000s?

=TRUNC(12543,-3)

10. Is this the same value you'd get if you rounded to the nearest 1000s?

No. That value, found using =ROUND(12543,-3) is 13000.

11. How does the INT function differ from the ROUND and TRUNC functions?

Like the ROUND and TRUNC functions, the INT function can also return the nearest integer value. ROUND and TRUNC can do more than this since you can specify at which point to round or truncate and INT is limited to just returning the nearest integer. Also, INT always rounds down to the nearest integer as opposed to TRUNC which simply chops off the decimal portion of a number and ROUND which will round up or down depending on which number is the closest. For positive values, INT and TRUNC return the same value but for negative values they never will.

12. How would you use the TRUNC function (and perhaps another function) to separate the number -12.345 into its integer and decimal components?

=TRUNC(-12.345) to get the integer and =ABS(-12.345-TRUNC(-12.345)) to get the decimal portion.

POWERS AND SQUARE ROOTS QUIZ
ANSWERS

1. What does it mean to raise a number to a power?

It means that you multiply a number by itself that specified number of times. So 3 raised to the power of 2 means that you multiply 3 times 3.

2. What function can be used to do this?

The POWER function.

3. Is there a way to do this with notation instead? How?

Yes. The carat $^\wedge$ will do the same thing.

4. Show how to take 5 to the power of 4 using both the function and the notation method.

=POWER(5,4)

=5^4

5. Can you use both of these methods to take a root power, such as the square root of a number? If so, write how to take the square root of 9.

=POWER(9,.5)
=9^.5

6. Is there a function that will specifically let you take the square root of a number? What is it? Apply it to 9.
Yes. SQRT. =SQRT(9)

7. What is the function that will let you return the value of Pi to fifteen digits?
PI

8. How would you write that?
=PI()

9. How would you calculate the area of a circle (which is Pi times the square of the radius) using the above functions where the radius is 3?
=PI()*(3^2)
=PI()*POWER(3,2)

10. What does the function SQRTPI give you?
The square root of a number times Pi.

11. If you wanted the square root of Pi itself, how could you get that value?
=PI()^.5
=SQRTPI(1)

LOGARITHMS QUIZ ANSWERS

**1. What formula would you use to obtain the value of
e?**

=EXP(1)

**2. What does the function used in the prior question
do?**

It returns the value *e* raised to the given power where *e*
is an irrational and transcendental number with an
approximate value of 2.718.

3. What is =LOG(100) asking?

It's asking what power you'd have to take the number
10 to in order to get a value of 100. In this case, the answer
is 2.

**4. Write a formula that uses the LOG function to
determine what power you'd have to take the number
2 to get a result of 24:**

=LOG(24,2)

**5. Write a formula that uses the LOG function to
determine what power you'd have to take *e* to to get a**

result of 24:
    =LOG(24,EXP(1))

6. Write a formula that uses the LN function to make the same determination:
    =LN(24)

7. What does the LN function do?
    It takes the natural logarithm of a number.

8. What does the LOG function do?
    It returns the logarithm of a number to the base you specify.

9. Which of the two is more flexible?
    The LOG function because it can perform the calculation the LN function does as well as use other bases.

10. What does the LOG10 function do?
    It returns the base ten logarithm of a number.

11. Should you use it?
    No need to because LOG will by default do the same thing.

FACTORIALS AND COMBINATIONS
QUIZ ANSWERS

1. What is the difference between permutations and combinations?

Permutations are ordered combinations. So with a permutations 123 and 321 are not the same. But with a combination they are because they both contain the same three values: 1, 2, and 3. If you were dividing ten people into teams of two, you'd want to use combinations because it doesn't matter if Gary is assigned to a group first or Bob is, at the end of the day you have a group that contains Gary and Bob. But if you were rank-ordering those same ten people then it does matter who is assigned first place, second place, etc. so you'd want to use permutations.

2. What does a factorial do?

It calculates the number of unique permutations you can generate given a specified sample size. So there are six permutations when you have three choices: 123, 132, 231, 213, 312, and 321.

3. What function in Excel will do this calculation for you?

FACT

4. What formula would you write to determine the number of possible permutations for a group of ten people?

=FACT(10)

5. What happens with the FACT function if you input a decimal value, for example =FACT(3.95)?

It will truncate the number provided and then do the factorial calculation. So in this case it would return the equivalent of =FACT(3).

6. What value will Excel return if you ask for the factorial of zero?

One.

7. What happens if you ask for the factorial of a negative number?

You'll get a #NUM! error message.

8. If you had a group of ten individuals and wanted to give out first, second, and third place medals, how would you use the FACT function to calculate the number of possible three-person outcomes?

=FACT(10)/FACT(10-3)

9. What if you instead wanted to calculate the number of three-person teams that could be built out of a population of nine people. What function would you use?

COMBIN

10. What does this function do?

It calculates the number of combinations for a given number of items.

11. How would you use it to calculate the number of two-person teams possible in a group of four individuals?

=COMBIN(4,2)

You can work this out on paper as well to check it. Your teams are 12, 13, 14, 23, 24, and 34.

12. What function would you use if you want to know the number of possible combinations where each possibility can be chosen multiple times? (In other words, you can have 22 as an outcome.)

COMBINA

13. So if you had a raffle drawing and there were ten people participating, each with one ticket and where each ticket was put back into the draw each time, and you wanted to know the odds of one person winning all three draws how would you do that calculation?

First calculate the total number of possible unique outcomes by using =COMBINA(10,3).

Then divide one (that's how many times one person would win all three draws) by the total number of possible outcomes to get the percentage of times that one person would've been expected to win all three raffles.

PRESENT AND FUTURE VALUES QUIZ ANSWERS

1. If you want to know the current value of a series of identical payments that you'll receive on an annual basis in the future, what function can you use to calculate that?

PV

2. What are the inputs to this function?

Rate: This is the rate you'll be paid (or pay) per period

Nper: This is the number of payment periods

Pmt: This is the amount you will receive or pay for each period

Fv: Is a lump sum payment that you'll receive or pay out at the very end of all payment periods

Type: Dictates when payments are made, either at the beginning of the payment period or at the end of the payment period. By default the assumption is that payments will be made at the end of the period.

3. What does the NPV function do?

Returns the net present value of an investment based

on a discount rate and a series of future cash flows (either incoming or outgoing).

4. What is the advantage of the NPV function over the PV function?

With the NPV function your payments can be different amounts whereas the PV function requires that the periodic payments be the same amount each period.

5. What limitation do both PV and NPV share?

The time period between each inflow or outflow must be the same.

6. If I have a range of values in Cells B2 through B8 that represent annual payments that I'm going to receive starting one year from now and want to calculate the net present value of those amounts using a ten percent annual interest rate, how would I write that:

=NPV(.1,B2:B8)

7. What if I'm going to receive $1,000 each year for the next five years and the annual interest rate is 10%. What formula would you write to calculate the current value of those future payments?

=PV(.1,5,1000)

You could also write a formula using NPV, such as =NPV(0.1,B2:B6), and get the same result.

8. What does the FORECAST function do?

It calculates a value for y given a specified value for x and existing known values for x and y. Predictions are made assuming a linear trend.

9. Why is it important to remember that it only works with a linear trend?

Because many relationships that occur in life are not in

fact linear and so the forecasted value will not necessarily be accurate.

10. Because of this, what should you do before using the FORECAST function?

Plot your data to see if it's following a linear or near linear trend. If it isn't, don't use FORECAST. Note that there is another forecasting function available starting with Excel 2016 that you can use instead in those instances.

11. What are the order of the inputs to the FORECAST function?

You list the x you want Excel to use in its prediction, then a range for all of the known y values, and then a corresponding range for all of the known x values.

12. Can you use FORECAST to predict a value prior to your data range? In other words, what y would be at a smaller value of x than is shown in your data table?

Yes. Just be careful if you've converted any time range (such as months) to a number for purposes of using the function because it will consider the 0 point as a point within the range.

THE FREQUENCY FUNCTION QUIZ ANSWERS

1. What does the FREQUENCY function do?

It takes a list of values and calculates how many occurrences of those values fall within ranges specified by the user.

2. What must you have in order to use the FREQUENCY function?

A series of "bin" values for the function to use so that it knows how to define each range.

3. What does it mean that FREQUENCY is an array function?

That it will return more than one value. This means that you have to highlight the cells where you want your answers returned first, then you type the formula in the first cell of the range, and then you use Ctrl+Shift+Enter to finish the calculation.

4. What are the inputs to the FREQUENCY function?

Data Array: This is the range of cells that include the data whose frequency you want to calculate.

Bins Array: This is the range of cells that define the bins you want to use for the calculation.

5. How is a bins array entry structured? And how is it used by Excel?

Each bin in the array is a single numeric value entered in a cell. For the first cell in a bins array, Excel will calculate the number of cells in the data array that have a value less than or equal to that value. For the next cell it will calculate the number of cells that have a value greater than the last one but less than or equal to the current cell. And so on. The final bins array, if it's blank will be used to calculate any entries greater than the last specified value.

6. What is an easy way to get a list of bin array values that correspond to all potential values in your data set?

Copy and paste those values into a new range and then use the Remove Duplicates option under Data Tools in the Data tab to get a list of unique values from the original range.

7. If the range of values you want to evaluate are in Column C and your bins values are in Cells D2 through D6, how would you write the formula to calculate your frequencies for each of those bin values?

=FREQUENCY(C:C,D2:D6)

THE HOW EXCEL HANDLES DATES
QUIZ ANSWERS

1. By default what does the number 1 represent with respect to a date in Excel?

The date January 1, 1900. It can also represent the value for a single day.

2. Can Excel handle dates prior to 1900?

No.

3. Can you use addition and subtraction with dates in Excel? Why or why not?

Yes. Because each date in Excel is treated like a number, you can use addition and subtraction with dates in Excel.

4. What is a serial_number with respect to date functions in Excel?

The numeric value for a date. In many functions this can also just be a reference to the date itself.

5. How does Excel handle dates differently on the Mac operating system? What does this mean for someone working between a PC and a Mac using Excel?

On Macs the beginning date is not January 1, 1900 but is instead January 2, 1904. That means there is a difference of 1,462 days between the value assigned to a specific date in Excel on a PC and that same date on a Mac.

6. How does Excel account for this?

Excel is set up to store dates according to one or the other system and that is specified in the File Options.

7. If you enter a two-digit year, for example '29, how will Excel treat that in terms of the century it applies?

For two-digit years between 00 and 29 it will interpret that as a date set in the 2000s, so 2000 to 2029. For two-digit years between 30 and 99 it will treat that as a date set in the 1900s, so 1930 to 1999.

DATE FUNCTIONS
QUIZ ANSWERS

1. What does the DATE function do?

It takes a specified year, month, and day of the month and returns a date. So =DATE(1900,1,1) will return a value of 1/1/1900. (Or whatever format you're using for your dates. If no date format automatically applies to a cell it will return the numeric value, in this case 1.)

2. What happens if you use the DATE function with a date prior to January 1, 1900, so for example if you use =DATE(1880,1,1)?

Excel will add the year value you provided to 1900 to provide the date. So =DATE(1880,1,1) becomes 1/1/3780.

3. Can you use a value for the month portion of the DATE function that is greater than 12? What about less than 1?

Yes. If you do so, Excel will take the year and day of the month provided and add that many months. If the number for months provided is negative it will subtract that many months, but it includes a value of zero as a legitimate month count. So =DATE(1905,-2,1) will go back to October 1, 1904 which is January minus three months.

4. What about days of the month? Can you have a number greater than 31 or a negative number?

Yes. It works the same way as the months do. It will carry forward that many days or if it goes backward it will go back that many days plus one additional day.

5. Write a formula that takes a date stored in Cell B2 and adds four months to it.

=DATE(YEAR(B2),MONTH(B2)+4,DAY(B2))

6. What does the YEAR function do?

It returns the year portion of a date in the integer range of 1900 through 9999.

7. How would you use YEAR to extract the year portion of the date March 1, 2010?

=YEAR("March, 1, 2010")
=YEAR("3/1/2010")
=YEAR("3-1-2010")
=YEAR(A1) where A1 contains the date

8. What happens if you fail to use quotation marks around a date used in a YEAR function?

You will get a #NUM! error message.

9. What does the MONTH function do?

It returns the month portion of a date in numeric form where January is represented by the number 1 and December is represented by the number 12.

10. What result will you get from =MONTH("April, 1, 1952")?

4

11. What does the DAY function do?

It returns the day portion of a date in numeric form from 1 to 31.

12. What does the HOUR function do?

It returns the hour component of a date/time in numeric form from 0 (which represents midnight) to 23 (which represents eleven o'clock in the evening).

13. What will =HOUR(NOW()) give you?

The current hour. For me it's currently five o'clock at night, so that value would be 17.

14. Since Excel treats dates as numbers, what is the value of an hour under Excel's system?

.041667 which is the equivalent of 1/24

15. Will you get a result with =HOUR(.166667)?

Yes. It will return a value of 4.

16. How does the MINUTE function work?

It returns the minute portion of a date/time in numeric form from 0 to 59.

17. Since Excel treats dates as numbers, what is the value of a minute under Excel's system?

.000694 or 1/60 of 1/24

18. What does the SECOND function do?

Returns the second portion of a date/time in the range from 0 to 59.

19. What result will you get from =SECOND("12:32:21")?

21

20. Since Excel treats dates as numbers, what is the value of a second under Excel's system?

.000011574 or 1/60 of 1/60 of 1/24

21. If you enter a date without entering a specific time of day and then use the HOUR, MINUTE, or SECOND function on that date, what value will Excel give you?

0

22. What does the WEEKDAY function do?

It returns the day of the week for a specified date using a value of 1 through 7 where the day of the week represented by each number is dependent upon the setting specified by the user.

23. What is the default setting for the WEEKDAY function in terms of numbering the days of the week?

By default, 1 will equal Sunday and so on until 7 equals Saturday.

24. If August 13, 2019 is a Tuesday and I use =WEEKDAY("August 13, 2019") what value will I get back?

3

25. What portion of the WEEKDAY function should you change if you want the numbers returned to map to different days of the week? How would you change the above formula so that Monday is treated as a 1 and Tuesday returns a value of 2 instead?

The optional return_type variable lets you specify which day of the week is considered the first day of the week. To change =WEEKDAY("August 13, 2019") so that Monday is the first day of the week and any Tuesday is a value of 2 you would write =WEEKDAY("August 13, 2019",2) or =WEEKDAY("August 13, 2019",11)

26. What does the following formula do:
=IF(WEEKDAY(A1,2)>5,12.95,9.95)

It says that if the date in Cell A1 using a numbering standard where Monday is 1 through to Sunday is 7 is greater than 5 (so a Saturday or Sunday) then return a value of 12.95. If it is 5 or less (so Monday through Friday) then return a value of 9.95.

27. What does the WEEKNUM function do?

It returns a number for which week in the year a date is part of. However, it returns values up to 53.

28. How does Excel define a week for purposes of the WEEKNUM function?

That depends on the return_type you choose. The default is for Excel to define a week as starting on a Sunday and to only include dates for that given year. So, for example, for 2019 week 1 was January 1st, a Tuesday, through January 5th, a Saturday. This can be adjusted so that any day of the week is considered the start point.

29. How do you get Excel to define a week in accordance with ISO standards when using the WEEKNUM function? And how does it work?

By setting the return_type value to 21. Excel takes the first week of the year that has a Thursday in it and starts the week on the Monday of that week even if the Monday of that week falls in the prior year.

30. What is another function you can use to get Excel to apply the ISO standard when determining the week number? And when did it become available?

ISOWEEKNUM which became available in Excel 2013

DATE CALCULATION FUNCTIONS IN EXCEL QUIZ ANSWERS

1. What does the DAYS function do?

It takes a given start date and a given end date and calculates the difference between them in terms of the number of days.

2. Do you need the DAYS function to do this?

No. You can also just use simple subtraction and put the dates in quote marks. For example, ="12/25/18"-"6/1/18" or =B1-C1 where the dates are stored in those cells.

3. What does the DAYS360 function do?

The DAYS360 function calculates the number of days between two dates assuming that all months have thirty days in them. (This is useful in some financial calculations.)

4. Are there different methods with DAYS360 for handling the last day of the month when it's either in February or in a month with 31 days?

Yes. The default is the U.S. or NASD method but you can also set it to use the European method.

5. What does the EDATE function do?

The EDATE function returns the serial number of the date that is the indicated number of months before or after the specified start date.

6. What is another way to get this same result?

Use the DATE function to extract YEAR, MONTH, and DAY from a date and then add the desired number of months to the MONTH value.

7. If I use =EDATE("March 1, 2019",4) what result will that give me?

43647 which is equivalent to July 1, 2019 because it takes that date and moves the month portion only forward the specified number of months. If I were to take that date and add 120 days to it, four months times thirty days, I would get a different result.

8. How does EDATE handle partial month values, such as =EDATE("March 1, 2019",4.9)?

It truncates the provided value, so this would be the equivalent of =EDATE("March 1, 2019",4)

9. What does the EOMONTH function do?

Returns the last day of the month before or after a specified number of months in serial number format.

10. What do you need to do with the result of an EDATE or EOMONTH formula?

Format it as a date because it will be a number until you do.

WORKDAYS AND NETWORKDAYS
QUIZ ANSWERS

1. What does the NETWORKDAYS function do?

It allows you to calculate the number of whole workdays between two dates.

2. How is this different from just using the DAYS function?

The DAYS function treats all days as the same. The NETWORKDAYS function will not include weekend days. However, the NETWORKDAYS function does count the start date and end date provided in its calculation whereas the DAYS function doesn't include the start date.

3. How can you incorporate holidays into the NETWORKDAYS function?

By using the optional third input for holidays. You can either provide a list of the holidays within curvy brackets { } or you can put the dates into a table and reference their location as your third input.

4. What if you don't want NETWORKDAYS to include the start date and the end date in the calculation?

You can follow the NETWORKDAYS function portion with subtraction to take out either the start date only (-1) or both the start and end dates (-2) from the count.

5. Using NETWORKDAYS write a formula calculating the number of workdays between August 28, 2019 and September 4, 2019 where September 2, 2019 is a holiday and you don't want to count the first or the last day in the count:

=NETWORKDAYS("8/28/19","9/4/19","9/2/19")-2

The answer is 3. There are a few other ways to write it, but this is one example.

6. What function would you use to calculate workdays if your weekend days are not Saturday and Sunday?

NETWORKDAYS.INTL

7. With which version of Excel did this function become available?

Excel 2010

8. Explain what the weekend input to the NETWORKDAYS.INTL function does:

It allows you to specify a custom weekend parameter. You can have a "weekend" that is only one day of the week or a weekend that consists of any two continuous days within the week by using this input. The values are listed in a dropdown menu.

9. Are NETWORKDAYS and NETWORKDAYS.INTL directly interchangeable? Can you just change one to the other and have it work?

No. Not if you used the holidays input for either function or the weekend input for the NETWORKDAYS.INTL function, because the third input for NETWORKDAYS is the list of holidays but that's the fourth input in the NETWORKDAYS.INTL function.

10. What does the WORKDAY function do?

It returns the value for the date that is before or after a specified number of workdays.

11. Does WORKDAY include the start date in its count like NETWORKDAYS does?

No.

12. What does the WORKDAY.INTL function do?

It returns the value for the date that is before or after a specified number of workdays but also allows for custom weekend parameters.

13. Let's say that your team is working six-day weeks and that they're allowed to have Wednesdays off. It's currently August 23, 2019 and your team says they need twelve more days to finish the project. There is a holiday on September 2, 2019. When will they complete the project?

September 7, 2019

$$=WORKDAY.INTL("August 23, 2019",12,14, "September 2, 2019")$$

14. What if they tell you this on the morning of the 23rd and you know that they'll be working all day so it will count towards their timeline. Will this impact the completion date?

Yes. Because WORKDAY and WORKDAY.INTL do not count the current date in their calculations.

September 6, 2019

=WORKDAY.INTL("August 23, 2019",11,14,
"September 2, 2019")

15. Can you create a custom set of off days using the WORKDAY.INTL function? How?

Yes. By inputting a binary string of values that shows which days are "on" and which days are "off" days where off days are shown using a 1 and on days are shown using a 0.

COMBINING FUNCTIONS
QUIZ ANSWERS

1. Is it possible to write a formula that uses more than one function?

Absolutely.

2. How would you write a formula that returns a value of TRUE if the value in Cell A1 is greater than 10 or the value in Cell B1 is greater than 10 and a value of FALSE otherwise?

=IF(OR(A1>10,B1>10),TRUE(),FALSE())

Note that that used four different functions in one formula.

3. What do you need to be careful about when combining functions together in one formula?

That you have all of your parens in the right place and don't forget any.

4. Do you need to use an equals sign in front of each function name when you combine functions in a single formula?

No. You just need to start your formula with an equals sign, but that's it.

5. What should you explore further if you're running into file size issues because of repeat calculations in your Excel worksheet?

Array formulas.

WHEN THINGS GO WRONG
QUIZ ANSWERS

1. Name five different error messages you might see.

#REF!, #VALUE!, #DIV/0!, #N/A, #NUM!

You also might see a comment that you've created a circular references or have too few arguments or that the formula you've written doesn't work and Excel wants to fix it for you.

2. What does #REF! generally indicate?

That you've deleted a value that was being referenced in that cell. For example, =A1+B1 will generate that message if you delete Column A or Column B.

3. How can you see where the cell that was deleted was located in your formula?

Click on the cell and look in the formula bar or double-click on the cell. The cell reference that's missing will have been replaced with #REF!.

4. What does a #VALUE! message indicate?

That the cell you're referencing is the wrong type of cell for that function. So maybe you have a date or number formatted as plain text, for example. In rare cases it could also mean that you have regional settings that impact how you're supposed to write your functions. It can also mean that you're referencing a now unavailable outside data source.

5. What does a #DIV/0! message indicate?

That you're dividing by zero or a blank cell.

6. If the #DIV/0! message is legitimate because nothing has been entered yet, what's a quick way to suppress it?

Use an IF function in that cell rather than just a division formula. So instead of having =A1/B1, have =IF(B1<>0,A1/B1,"").

7. What does a #N/A error message generally mean?

That Excel isn't finding what it was asked to look for.

8. What can you check for if this happens and you don't think it should have?

Check the formatting of your values to make sure they match. Also check that there aren't extra spaces in one of your inputs or lookup values.

9. What does the IFERROR function do? What do you need to be careful with if you use it?

Suppresses an error result and replaces it with a zero, a blank space, or text that you provide. It will suppress all error messages, even ones you may want to see.

10. What does the #NUM! error message generally indicate?

That there are numeric values in a function that are not valid. It also happens when the function is going to return a result that is too large or too small or can't find a solution.

11. What is a circular reference?

One that references itself. So if in Cell A1 I write =A1+B1 that is circular because to generate the answer in Cell A1 I would have to use the value in Cell A1. That would create a continuous loop if you actually tried to do it.

12. If you don't think you have a circular reference but Excel tells you you do, what should you check for?

That you haven't created an indirect circular reference. For example, if you write in Cell A1 =B1+C1 that looks fine. But if the value in C1 is calculated by =SUM(A:A) then you're using the value in Cell A1 to calculate the value in Cell C1 and can't also use it to calculate the value in Cell A1.

13. If you're trying to figure out what cells are feeding the value in a cell where can you go to do that?

Trace Precedents under Formula Auditing in the Formulas tab.

14. If Excel tells you you have too few arguments, what should you check for?

First, that you've included all required inputs for that particular function. In the function description anything listed with brackets is optional, but anything listed as text without brackets is not. Also, check that you have all of your parens and commas and quotation marks in the right places.

15. What can you do with a formula that just isn't working the way it should be?

Double-click on the formula and check that all of the cell references are pointing to the right cells. Also, if you're copying a formula make sure that you used $ signs to lock any cell references that need to be locked. Also make sure that any options for that function were chosen properly. (Exact versus approximate, ascending vs. descending, etc.)

(And one that isn't in the guide, but came up as I was writing this, if you copied from Word into Excel make sure that you replace any curly quotes or smart quotes with straight quotes. Excel will not accept smart quotes.)

CELL NOTATION
QUIZ ANSWERS

1. What is Cell A1 referencing?

The cell that's in Column A and Row 1.

2. Name two ways you can reference more than one cell in a function.

With a comma between individual cells, row references, or column references. Or with a colon to reference a range of cells, rows, or columns.

For example:

=SUM(A1, B1, C1)

or

=SUM(A:A,B:B,C:C)

or

=SUM(1:1,2:2,3:3)

or

=SUM(A1:C1)

or

=SUM(A:C)

or

=SUM(1:3)

3. Can you reference a cell in another worksheet?

Yes. You just need to include the worksheet name reference as well.

4. Can you reference a cell in another workbook?

Yes. You just need to include the workbook name reference as well, but be careful doing so because the formula may not work if that other workbook is moved, renamed, or deleted.

5. What's an easy way to reference a cell in another worksheet or workbook?

Start your formula and then just click on the cell you need. Excel will write the cell reference for you.

BONUS: EXERCISES

EXERCISE 1

Take the following data and calculate

	A	B	C	D
1	**Customer Name**	**Units**	**Price**	**Product**
2	Albert Jones	5	$2.50	Widgets
3	Mark Smith	10	$5.00	Whatsits
4	Nancy Baker	5	$2.50	Whatsits
5	Albert Jones	10	$5.00	Whatsits
6	Mark Smith	5	$5.00	Whatsits
7	Nancy Baker	5	$5.00	Whatsits
8	Albert Jones	4	$5.00	Widgets
9	Mark Smith	3	$2.50	Widgets
10	Nancy Baker	2	$2.50	Widgets

1. The total spent for each transaction.

2. The total number of units sold.

3. The total amount earned using SUMPRODUCT.

4. The average price per unit across the transactions.

5. Build a grid from that data that has customer name in rows and product across the top and calculate:
   A. Amount spent per customer per product.
   B. Number of units ordered per customer per product.
   C. Average unit price paid per transaction per customer per product.

EXERCISE 2

1. Take the following numbers and calculate the average, median, and mode.

2. Also calculate the mode.mult with room for four possible results.

10

10

10

20

50

300

300

300

40

50

1200

1200

1200

50

EXERCISE 3

Take the following data table and combine the entries to form a single entry with last name, first name middle name for each row with no additional spaces and the name in all caps. Do this in one formula for each entry.

	A	B	C
1	**First Name**	**Middle Name**	**Last Name**
2	Amanda	Diane	Cook
3	Mark	David	Allen
4	Brad		Jones
5	Alejandro		Sanchez

EXERCISE 4

1. Build a simple discount table that gives customers $5 off if they spend $25 or more and $10 off if they spend $50 or more and then write a VLOOKUP function to find the discount for purchases of $5, $25, $45, $50, and $75.

2. Do the same with a nested IF function.

EXERCISE 5

Using the following numbers answer the following questions:

10

12

14

5

8

7

16

20

22

34

1. Looking from smallest value to largest value, what place in the order is 8?

2. Looking from largest value to smallest value, what place in the order is 22?

3. What value is the 6th smallest value?

4. What value is the 4th largest value?

5. How could you calculate a random whole number that is between the smallest value in this range and the largest value in this range using one formula to calculate the smallest and largest value as well as the random number?

EXERCISE 6

You have a project that you are managing. The start date of the project is July 1, 2019 and will need to be finished by August 30, 2019. Assume the only holiday is July 4, 2019.

1. Assuming a standard U.S. workweek with Saturdays and Sundays off, how many days will this give you to complete the project?

2. The team lead for the first leg of the project says that she needs fifteen working days to complete her portion. What day should you expect her to be completed by assuming her team will begin work on July 1st.

3. Assume that you have ten people assigned to this project and that you want to put them into two teams of five. How many possible team configurations do you have to choose from?

4. The project requires completing 500 widgets during the project period. Assuming that in the first three weeks you produce 68, 84, and 72 widgets, respectively, and

that this phase of the project has six weeks for completion, and that there will be no significant changes to the production rate, will you reach your goal? If not, approximately how many widgets will you have produced by the end of the six-week period?

EXERCISE 7

Take the following table of units sold by each of three sales people for each of three products.

	A	B	C	D
1		Jane	Javier	Mo
2	Widgets	25	22	24
3	Whatchamacallits	15	18	30
4	Thingies	12	20	15

1. Build a table that lists the salesperson name in rows and the product name in each column and remains linked to the original table of data.

2. Write a formula that will look in the original table for the number of Whatchamacallits sold by Javier using a search for Javier's name.

3. Write a formula that will look in the original table for the number of Whatchamacallits sold by Javier assuming that you won't know which column Javier is

in nor will you know which column Whatchamacallits
are in.

EXERCISE 8

1. Take the following value in Cell A1, $121/hr, and
    write a formula that will extract the dollar portion of
    the entry only.

2. Write a formula to calculate at what point in the above
    entry the / starts?

3. You have a cube that is 2 foot by 2 foot by 2 foot.
    Write a formula to calculate the area of that cube in
    feet using exponents. Write a formula to calculate the
    area of the cube in meters.

EXERCISE 9

1. Write a formula to calculate how often each of the following values occurs: 2, 2, 2, 6, 6, 6, 6, 8, 8, 9, 9, 9, 9

EXERCISE 10

1. Assume that you're thinking of buying a car. Your options are to pay $5,500 now or to pay monthly payments of $125 per month for the next four years. Assuming that the relative interest rate is 5%, which should you choose to do?

2. Which is better: To pay $5,000 now or to pay $5,250 in five years assuming there's a 10% rate per year?

3. What amount would you have to invest today to generate $5,250 in five years assuming a 10% rate per year?

4. How does that combine with your answer to the question before it?

BONUS:
EXERCISE ANSWERS

EXERCISE 1

Take the following data and calculate

	A	B	C	D
1	**Customer Name**	**Units**	**Price**	**Product**
2	Albert Jones	5	$2.50	Widgets
3	Mark Smith	10	$5.00	Whatsits
4	Nancy Baker	5	$2.50	Whatsits
5	Albert Jones	10	$5.00	Whatsits
6	Mark Smith	5	$5.00	Whatsits
7	Nancy Baker	5	$5.00	Whatsits
8	Albert Jones	4	$5.00	Widgets
9	Mark Smith	3	$2.50	Widgets
10	Nancy Baker	2	$2.50	Widgets

* * *

	A	B	C	D	E
1	**Customer Name**	**Units**	**Price**	**Product**	**Total Spen**
2	Albert Jones	5	$2.50	Widgets	$12.50
3	Mark Smith	10	$5.00	Whatsits	$50.00
4	Nancy Baker	5	$2.50	Whatsits	$12.50
5	Albert Jones	10	$5.00	Whatsits	$50.00
6	Mark Smith	5	$5.00	Whatsits	$25.00
7	Nancy Baker	5	$5.00	Whatsits	$25.00
8	Albert Jones	4	$5.00	Widgets	$20.00
9	Mark Smith	3	$2.50	Widgets	$7.50
10	Nancy Baker	2	$2.50	Widgets	$5.00
11	**Total**	49			**$207.50**
12					
13					
14	Avg Price Per Unit Per Trans	$3.89	SUMPRODUCT		$207.50
15					

1. The total spent for each transaction.

Formula for Cell E2 is

=B2*C2

This can be copied down to the rest of the rows in the table.

2. The total number of units sold.

Formula in B11 is

=SUM(B2:B10)

This can also be created using the AutoSum option.

3. The total amount earned using SUMPRODUCT.

The formula to calculate the total amount earned using SUMPRODUCT is

=SUMPRODUCT(B2:B10,C2:C10)

4. The average price per unit across the transactions.

To calculate the average of the per unit prices paid across the transaction you can use the formula:

=AVERAGE(C2:C10)

5. Build a grid from that data that has customer name in rows and product across the top and calculate:

	H	I	J
1	**Amount Spent**	Whatsits	Widgets
2	Albert Jones	$ 50.00	$ 32.50
3	Mark Smith	$ 75.00	$ 7.50
4	Nancy Baker	$ 37.50	$ 5.00
5			
6	**Units Ordered**	Whatsits	Widgets
7	Albert Jones	10	9
8	Mark Smith	15	3
9	Nancy Baker	10	2
10			
11	**Average Unit Price**	Whatsits	Widgets
12	Albert Jones	$5.00	$3.75
13	Mark Smith	$5.00	$2.50
14	Nancy Baker	$3.75	$2.50

A. Amount spent per customer per product.

Assuming customer name is in Column H and product is in Row 1 as shown in the solution above, in Cell I2 write the formula

=SUMIFS($E:$E,$A:$A,$H2,$D:D,I1)

and then copy it to the rest of the cells in the table.

B. Number of units ordered per customer per product.

Assuming customer name is in Column H and product is in Row 6 as shown in the solution above, in Cell I7 write the formula

=SUMIFS($B:$B,$A:$A,$H7,$D:D,I6)

and then copy it to the rest of the cells in the table.

C. Average unit price paid per transaction per customer per product.

Assuming customer name is in Column H and product is in Row 11 as shown in the solution above, in Cell I12 write the formula

=AVERAGEIFS($C:$C,$A:$A,$H12,$D:D,I11)

and then copy it to the rest of the cells in the table.

EXERCISE 2

1. Take the following numbers and calculate the average, median, and mode.

2. Also calculate the mode.mult with room for four possible results.

10

10

10

20

50

300

300

300

40

50

1200

1200

1200

50

* * *

	A	B	C	D
1	10			
2	10		Average	338.5714
3	10		Median	50
4	20		Mode	10
5	50			10
6	300		Mode.Mult	50
7	300			300
8	300			1200
9	40			
10	50			
11	1200			
12	1200			
13	1200			
14	50			

1. To calculate the average, median, and mode with the values in Cells A1 through A14 use:

=AVERAGE(A1:A14)

=MEDIAN(A1:A14)

=MODE(A1:A14)

2. To calculate the multiple mode outcome:

   A. Select Cells D5 through D8
   B. Use =MODE.MULT(A1:A14)
   C. Finish with Ctrl + Shift + Enter rather than enter.

EXERCISE 3

Take the following data table and combine the entries to form a single entry with last name, first name middle name for each row with no additional spaces and the name in all caps. Do this in one formula for each entry.

	A	B	C
1	**First Name**	**Middle Name**	**Last Name**
2	Amanda	Diane	Cook
3	Mark	David	Allen
4	Brad		Jones
5	Alejandro		Sanchez

* * *

	A	B	C	D
1	**First Name**	**Middle Name**	**Last Name**	**Last, First Middle**
2	Amanda	Diane	Cook	COOK, AMANDA DIANE
3	Mark	David	Allen	ALLEN, MARK DAVID
4	Brad		Jones	JONES, BRAD
5	Alejandro		Sanchez	SANCHEZ, ALEJANDRO

One way to do this is to use the formula

=UPPER(TRIM(CONCATENATE(C2,", ",A2," ",B2)))

You could also do it with the TRIM and UPPER functions in different positions within the formula.

EXERCISE 4

1. Build a simple discount table that gives customers $5 off if they spend $25 or more and $10 off if they spend $50 or more and then write a VLOOKUP function to find the discount for purchases of $5, $25, $45, $50, and $75.

2. Do the same with a nested IF function.

* * *

Here is one possible way to structure the problem:

A. Build a discount table in Cells A1 through B5 with the values in Cells A3 through B5.

B. Place the test values in Cells A8 through A12.

	A	B	C	D
1	**Discount Table**			
2	**Purchase Amount**	**Discount**		
3	$0.00	$0.00		
4	$25.00	$5.00		
5	$50.00	$10.00		
6				
7	**Test Amounts**	**VLOOKUP**	**IF Function**	
8	$5.00	$0.00	$0.00	
9	$25.00	$5.00	$5.00	
10	$45.00	$5.00	$5.00	
11	$50.00	$10.00	$10.00	
12	$75.00	$10.00	$10.00	
13				
14	**Row 8 Formulas**			
15	**VLOOKUP**	=VLOOKUP(A8,$A$3:$B$5,2)		
16	**IF Function**	=IF(A8<$A$4,$B$3,IF(A8<$A$5,$B$4,$B$5))		

1. In Row 8 for the VLOOKUP function you can then write the formula:

$$=VLOOKUP(A8,\$A\$3:\$B\$5,2)$$

and copy it down to the rest of the cells. Because of the \$ signs in the formula it will continue to work for all rows.

2. In Row 8 for the IF function you can then write the formula:

$$=IF(A8<\$A\$4,\$B\$3,IF(A8<\$A\$5,\$B\$4,\$B\$5))$$

and copy that down to the rest of the cells and because of the \$ signs it will also continue to work for all rows.

EXERCISE 5

Using the following numbers answer the following questions:

$$10$$
$$12$$
$$14$$
$$5$$
$$8$$
$$7$$
$$16$$
$$20$$
$$22$$
$$34$$

* * *

The formulas given below assume you entered the values in Cells A1 through A10, but the results should be the same no matter where you entered the values.

1. Looking from smallest value to largest value, what place in the order is 8?

3rd. You can use =RANK(8,A1:A10,1) to calculate this.

2. Looking from largest value to smallest value, what place in the order is 22?

2nd. You can use =RANK(22,A1:A10) to calculate this.

3. What value is the 6th smallest value?

14. You can use =SMALL(A1:A10,6) to calculate this.

4. What value is the 4th largest value?

16. You can use =LARGE(A1:A10,4) to calculate this.

5. How could you calculate a random whole number that is between the smallest value in this range and the largest value in this range using one formula to calculate the smallest and largest value as well as the random number?

Using

=RANDBETWEEN(SMALL(A1:A10,1),LARGE(A1:A10,1))

EXERCISE 6

You have a project that you are managing. The start date of the project is July 1, 2019 and will need to be finished by August 30, 2019. Assume the only holiday is July 4, 2019.

1. **Assuming a standard U.S. workweek with Saturdays and Sundays off, how many days will this give you to complete the project?**

   44
   =NETWORKDAYS("July 1, 2019","August 30, 2019","July 4, 2019")

2. **The team lead for the first leg of the project says that she needs fifteen working days to complete her portion. What day should you expect her to be completed by assuming her team will begin work on July 1st.**

   July 22, 2019
   =WORKDAY("July 1, 2019",15-1,"July 4, 2019")

3. **Assume that you have ten people assigned to this project and that you want to put them into two teams of five. How many possible team configurations do you have to choose from?**

    252

    =COMBIN(10,5)

4. **The project requires completing 500 widgets during the project period. Assuming that in the first three weeks you produce 68, 84, and 72 widgets, respectively, and that this phase of the project has six weeks for completion, and that there will be no significant changes to the production rate, will you reach your goal? If not, approximately how many widgets will you have produced by the end of the six-week period?**

No. Approximately 466 widgets will be produced. This can be calculated using the FORECAST function to predict output for weeks four, five, and six.

For the first three weeks we have 224 widgets. If you then put those into a table, say in Cells A1 through B4 where Column A has the week number and Column B has the number of widgets made in that week, you can then use FORECAST to predict the number of widgets produced in weeks 4, 5, and 6, respectively.

=FORECAST(4,$B$2:$B$4,$A$2:$A$4)

=FORECAST(5,$B$2:$B$4,$A$2:$A$4)

=FORECAST(6,$B$2:$B$4,$A$2:$A$4)

The values predicted are 78.67, 80.67, and 82.67 which when added to the 224 from the first three weeks is approximately 466 widgets.

	A	B	C
1	Week	Widgets	
2	1	68	
3	2	84	
4	3	72	
5			
6			FORECAST
7	Week	Widgets	Formula
8	4	78.66667	=FORECAST(4,$B$2:$B$4,$A$2:$A$4)
9	5	80.66667	=FORECAST(5,$B$2:$B$4,$A$2:$A$4)
10	6	82.66667	=FORECAST(6,$B$2:$B$4,$A$2:$A$4)

EXERCISE 7

Take the following table of units sold by each of three sales people for each of three products.

	A	B	C	D
1		Jane	Javier	Mo
2	Widgets	25	22	24
3	Whatchamacallits	15	18	30
4	Thingies	12	20	15

1. Build a table that lists the salesperson name in rows and the product name in each column and remains linked to the original table of data.

This can be done easily with the TRANSPOSE function. Highlight an area that is four cells by four cells, type =TRANSPOSE(A1:D4) in the first cell while the others remain highlighted, and then use Ctrl+Shift+Enter to populate the four cells. To remove the 0 value in the top left corner of the table you can go to the corresponding cell in the original table and type ="" into that cell and then hit Enter.

2. **Write a formula that will look in the original table for the number of Whatchamacallits sold by Javier using a search for Javier's name.**

   =HLOOKUP("Javier",A1:D4,3)

3. **Write a formula that will look in the original table for the number of Whatchamacallits sold by Javier assuming that you won't know which column Javier is in nor will you know which column Whatchamacallits are in:**

   =INDEX(A1:D4,MATCH("Whatchamacallits",A1:A
   4,0),MATCH("Javier",A1:D1,0))

EXERCISE 8

1. Take the following value in Cell A1, $121/hr, and
    write a formula that will extract the dollar portion
    of the entry only.

    =LEFT(A1,LEN(A1)-LEN("/hr"))

2. Write a formula to calculate at what point in the
    above entry the / starts?

    =SEARCH("/",A1)

3. You have a cube that is 2 foot by 2 foot by 2 foot.
    Write a formula to calculate the area of that cube
    in feet using exponents. Write a formula to
    calculate the area of the cube in meters.

    =2^3 or
    =POWER(2,3)

    =(CONVERT(2,"ft","m"))^3 or
    =CONVERT(POWER(2,3),"ft^3","m^3")

EXERCISE 9

1. **Write a formula to calculate how often each of the following values occurs: 2, 2, 2, 6, 6, 6, 6, 8, 8, 9, 9, 9, 9**

Put the values into one cell each to make a table. Copy those values to a new location and remove duplicates. (Or create your own table of the unique values.) Highlight the cells in the next column that are next to the unique values and use the FREQUENCY function to calculate occurrence of each one. This is an array function so be sure to use Ctrl+Shift+Enter instead of Enter.

	A	B	C	D
1	Entries		Value	Occurrence
2	2		2	3
3	2		6	4
4	2		8	2
5	6		9	4
6	6			
7	6			
8	6			
9	8			
10	8			
11	9			
12	9			
13	9			
14	9			

In this example, the formula was

=FREQUENCY(A2:A14,C2:C5)

since the original values were in Cells A2 through A14 and the unique values were in Cells C2 through C5.

EXERCISE 10

1. Assume that you're thinking of buying a car. Your options are to pay \$5,500 now or to pay monthly payments of \$125 per month for the next four years. Assuming that the relative interest rate is 5%, which should you choose to do?

You should take the payments.

Even though you pay \$6,000 for the entire term of the loan (125*48), the present value of those payments is only \$5,427 which is less than the \$5,500 you would pay out of pocket. This is calculated using

$$=-PV((0.05/12),48,125)$$

2. Which is better: To pay \$5,000 now or to pay \$5,250 in five years assuming there's a 10% rate per year?

Pay \$5,250 in five years. The net present value of \$5,250 in five years at a 10% rate is only \$3,105. This can be calculated using:

$$=NPV(0.1,0,0,0,0,5000) \text{ or } =5000/(1.1\text{^}5).$$

3. **What amount would you have to invest today to generate $5,250 in five years assuming a 10% rate per year?**

$3,259.84

You can calculate this using

=NPV(0.1,0,0,0,0,5250)

4. **How does that combine with your answer to the question before it?**

This means that you could take your $5,000 you have now, invest $3,260 worth of it at 10% to make that $5,250 payment in five years and spend the rest of it and still meet your obligation so it justifies choosing to pay the $5,250 in five years rather than $5,000 now.

INDEX OF QUIZZES

Quiz Name	Quiz	Answers
Quiz		
Date Functions Quiz	343	467
Date Calculation Functions In Excel Quiz	347	473
WORKDAYS And NETWORKDAYS Quiz	349	475
Combining Functions Quiz	351	479
When Things Go Wrong (Functions) Quiz	353	481
Cell Notation Quiz	355	485

ABOUT THE AUTHOR

M.L. Humphrey is a former stockbroker with a degree in Economics from Stanford and an MBA from Wharton who has spent close to twenty years as a regulator and consultant in the financial services industry.

You can reach M.L. at mlhumphreywriter@gmail.com or at mlhumphrey.com.